Praise for *Just A Minute*

Over the years that Wess Stafford and I have become good friends and ministry partners, one thing has become crystal clear: Wess's unbridled devotion to children, especially those in deep poverty, knows no boundaries. That's why *Just A Minute* is so pivotal. It will remind you who it was that launched your life—and who deserves your thanks. And more importantly, it issues an impassioned plea to make "just a minute" differences in the lives of the children all around you. I know of no better man to proclaim that today. . . right now is your moment to change a life forever.

MICHAEL W. SMITH
Singer/Songwriter

My dear friend, whom I lovingly call "Uncle Wess" has written a treasure of a book called *Just A Minute*. Full of incredibly moving stories, Wess's writing inspires us all to realize that every interaction with a child has the power to change his or her destiny. Wess's integrity, compassion, and love for Jesus has had a profound impact on my life. One cannot encounter him in person or in writing and not be changed. Prepare to be encouraged and moved!

REBECCA ST. JAMES
Singer, writer, and actress

Knowing how "in tune" Wess is with children, it doesn't surprise me that *Just A Minute* came straight from his heart and his experience. Wess has always been a champion for children, and in *Just A Minute* he makes us champions as well. Whether it is a special encounter or a lifelong commitment to child development, *Just A Minute* helps us all shape kids who will create healthier families, communities, and countries—not to mention finding their own special place in the world.

DR. GARY CHAPMAN
Author of the #1 New York Times bestselling book
The 5 Love Languages

Jesus called children "My little ones," and gave a stern warning to anyone who would cause a child to stumble. This book is a challenge for every follower of Jesus to take notice of the little ones in our midst, and to show them we love them because He first loved us.

BOB LEPINE
Cohost, FamilyLife Today

Every kid needs at least one person who is crazy about them. As an internationally recognized child advocate, Wess Stafford has given his life to helping children all over the world break free from poverty, in Jesus' name. In this fascinating read, *Just A Minute,* Stafford takes us on an incredible journey into the divine appointments and life-giving opportunities that God gives us every day. Enter its pages and you'll be forever changed!

DR. TIM CLINTON
President, American Association of Christian Counselors

In the Heart of a Child, One Moment . . .
Can Last Forever

JUST A MINUTE

WESS STAFFORD
President and CEO, Compassion International

WITH DEAN MERRILL

MOODY PUBLISHERS
CHICAGO

All Scripture quotations, unless otherwise indicated, are taken from the *Holy Bible, New International Version*®. NIV®. Copyright © 1973, 1978, 1984, 2011 by Biblica, Inc.™ Used by permission. All rights reserved worldwide.

Scripture quotations marked NLT are taken from the *Holy Bible, New Living Translation*, copyright © 1996, 2004. Used by permission of Tyndale House Publishers, Inc., Wheaton, Illinois 60189, U.S.A. All rights reserved.

Scripture quotations marked NKJV are taken from the *New King James Version*. Copyright © 1982 by Thomas Nelson, Inc. Used by permission. All rights reserved.

Edited by Elizabeth Cody Newenhuyse
Interior design: Smartt Guys design
Cover design: John Hamilton Design
Cover image: iStockPhoto, Photodisc, and courtesy of Compassion International

Library of Congress Cataloging-in-Publication Data

Stafford, Wess.
    Just a minute : in the heart of a child, one moment-- can last forever / Wess Stafford with Dean Merrill.
       p. cm.
    Includes bibliographical references.
    ISBN 978-0-8024-0472-5
    1. Caring—Religious aspects—Christianity. 2. Child care—Religious aspects,Christianity. 3. Church work with children. 4. Christian education of children. 5. Child psychology. 6. Children and adults. I. Merrill, Dean. II. Title.
    BV4647.S9.S73 2012
    259'.22—dc23

                                        2011036920

3 5 7 9 10 8 6 4 2

Printed in the United States of America

To the very next child

God brings across your path . . .

if only for just a minute.

More Praise for *Just A Minute*

Any of us who has ever pursued a career path, a life direction or a dream that seemed beyond the realm of possibility knows what a difference every word of encouragement made along the way. Wess's book reminds us that in the busyness of all of our lives we cannot forget the potential for each interaction we have with a child, whether it be our own children, a relative, a neighbor, or a complete stranger. Because of Compassion International, Wess Stafford is in a unique position of offering life and hope to children born in hopelessness. Whatever Wess Stafford has to say, I am ready to listen.

> AMY GRANT
> Singer, songwriter, and advocate for children

I can't think of anyone who's been a more consistent advocate and champion for the cause of caring, protecting, and investing in our children . . . especially those in the most vulnerable situations. In *Just a Minute*, Wess Stafford awakens us to see the vital role each of us can play in unleashing the infinite potential that resides in every child. *Just a Minute* inspires us to see children the way God does and shows us what can happen when we choose to seize the moments that come our way to breathe life and encouragement into a child. If you want to change the world for good . . . read it cover to cover!

> JIMMY MELLADO
> President, Willow Creek Association

I distinctly rememer the first "minute" when I met Wess Stafford and was encouraged by the heart of Christ in him. For this reason, I can't imagine a better person to write on the subject of maximizing our minutes to show the love of the Father in heaven to children all around us in the world.

> DAVID PLATT
> Senior Pastor, The Church at Brook Hills,
> Birmingham, Alabama, author of *Radical:*
> *Taking Back Your Faith from the American Dream*

CONTENTS

Introduction: The Power of a Minute   11

Section 1: **A Moment for Rescue**   19

    Errand of Mercy
    Plucked from the Burning
    Not Again?
    Little Jessica

Section 2: **A Moment to Build Self-Worth**   35

    Look at Those Shoes!
    The Wave Game
    Up from Despair
    "Only" a Girl
    Full Circle
    The Green Journal
    Fervent Fan
    The White Gardenia
    Apple of Her Eye
    Dancing for Grandpa

Section 3: **A Moment to Form Character**   **63**

The Greatest Fish

Owning Up to the Truth

The Storm Windows

The Casting Lesson

Short Talk on the Steps

Beautiful on the Inside

Make a Wish

Problem or Solution?

Race without a Finish

Section 4: **A Moment to Discover Talent**   **89**

"You Can't Sing"

To Be a Dork?

Hand on the Shoulder

Something's Missing

When Your Back Is Against the Wall

Surprise in the Drawer

Ears to Hear, Eyes to See

Section 5: **A Moment to Awaken the Spirit**   **111**

Invisible

Imporant Work to Do

The Boy Who Listened

A Tale of Two Blunders

Straight Talk

Benediction

A Giving Spirit

Out of the Flames, a Calling

Section 6: **A Moment to Stretch the Mind**   **137**

A Class of "Retards"

The Troublemaker

Nouns and Adverbs

Not So Dumb After All

Grandma's "Very Good" Reader

Spilled Milk

Mrs. Warren's Car

Three Minutes

Nurturing a Dream

Section 7: **A Moment to Realize One's Calling**   **157**

The Compass

Ultimate Sacrifice

Passing the Pen

The Chief's Speech

The Shoe Store

The Olive Seedling

Just Kidding Around?

Big Plans for a Small Girl

Wind Beneath Her Wings

Surprise Box

Course Correction

The Submarine Is All Yours

"Spell My Name, Please"

Conclusion: What Now?   **187**

Thank You   **213**

Notes   **217**

Introduction

THE POWER OF A MINUTE

"There's always one moment in childhood when the door opens and lets the future in." —Graham Greene

I never intended to write this book. I didn't go looking for it—it found me. Let me explain. My first book, *Too Small to Ignore,* was 266 pages long. But just three of those pages (9–12) form the genesis of this book, *Just a Minute.*

In the six years since the first book appeared, I've traveled across the world speaking, as always, about the value of children. It has often required me to tell my story of both joy and agony while growing up in West Africa. I've noticed that whenever I start talking about how tender and impressionable the heart of a child is, the auditorium goes eerily quiet. The metaphor of a child's spirit being a lot like wet cement or moist clay, just waiting for an act of kindness, a hug, or a well-timed word of encouragement, seems to bring a flood of memory to many listeners. I can see that momentarily I have "lost" them. Their eyes turn pensive, their gaze wanders somewhere beyond me, and they are children again, lost in their thoughts . . . remembering.

I sometimes ask the audience directly, "So who was it? What did they say to you? What did they do? Who believed in you before you believed in yourself?" Eyes well up with tears, and audible sobs have broken out. Once in Holland, I had to stop and comfort my translator, who broke down in the middle of our message.

> **I have become convinced that if God stands a child before you, for even just a minute, it is a divine appointment.**

After speaking engagements I have lingered sometimes for hours as people line up to tell me their stories. We laugh, cry, hug, and then part as kindred spirits. We are better, more grateful, more determined people for the moments spent together. Book signings have become emotional times of memories and gratitude. Meanwhile, emails have poured in from across the world in which readers share their reflections, who blessed them, and what they are now doing to pass on that blessing.

Divine Appointments

So this book simply had to be written. From the stories of others I have become convinced that if God stands a child before you, for even just a minute, it is a divine appointment. You have the chance to launch a life, if you will. You never know when you are making a memory.

With each child you encounter, you have the power and opportunity to build up . . . or, sadly, to tear down. A life can be literally launched with as little as a single word, an uplifting comment, a well-timed hug, a tender prayer, a compliment, the holding of a frightened hand, or the gentle wiping of a tear—all in just a minute!

And all of us, with no training, are qualified to do it. No one can say, "Well, children are just not my thing—I don't 'get' them. I don't know how to handle them, act around them, or relate to them." The truth is, you deserve an honorary doctorate in "childhood." You have done a minimum of eighteen years of "field research" in this complex subject. Having been a child yourself, you've experienced firsthand all there is to know about childhood—you may know what it feels like done right, or sadly, what it feels like done horribly wrong. You are who you are and act the way you do because of those years spent as a child.

Child development experts know that the most basic and strongest values, worldview, and self-perceptions are deeply entrenched within us at a very early age. Perhaps this is why the Scriptures so clearly and passionately call to us to "speak up for those who cannot speak for themselves" (Proverbs 31:8).

Stories, Stories . . .

But I don't intend to lecture you in this book. Instead, I'm going to tell stories—lots of them. I love stories. I grew up in an African village with no electricity, no TV or even radio (other than shortwave), so we gathered each evening around the village bonfire and told stories. Perhaps the most respected skill in my village in northern Ivory Coast was not hunting, fishing, or tilling the best field; it was the ability to tell a good story.

I think Jesus loved stories. No matter how important His message, He almost always embedded it in a story. Sometimes, much to His followers' dismay, the story was *all* that Jesus would tell them. Parables, He seemed to feel, deserved to be pondered and figured out over time.

Whether you are a toddler being tucked into bed, or you have three PhDs, you probably love and learn most from stories. Give me a wonderful, profound, three-point sermon, even with the outline printed in the church bulletin—and (is it just me?) by Wednesday of that week, I will remember only the jokes and any stories the preacher casually inserted to spice up the journey toward his more profound point, whatever it was. (Sorry, pastors.)

I have put these stories into seven sections that make sense together. But you will find that the good-news stories and the bad-news stories are intermingled, without warning—much like real life. We never know when we're making a lifelong memory for someone. That's why we have to be so gentle and kind to one another, all the time.

Perhaps someone once said to you, "My, but you have a beautiful voice"—and you seized that moment to the degree that singing is now your profession, or at least something you love doing for others. It all started with "just a minute."

Or somebody saw you do an act of kindness on the playground and took time to affirm you as a caring person. You may not remember the words spoken, but you have grown up to be a thoughtful, generous, sweet-spirited adult. It brings you great joy to bless others. It may now even be your profession.

Moments matter. Ask any actor—they can almost always tell you of the first stage where they stood. Their performance may have been a disaster, but the sound of applause gripped their heart. They've never forgotten the joy of making people laugh, or moving people emotionally. They were smitten in a minute, and now they never miss a chance to act.

In the pages that follow, we will enter the life stories of doctors, missionaries, soldiers, international leaders, sports heroes, politicians, and many more who all share one thing in common—they remember the "just a minute" that launched their extraordinary lives.

But you will also read about the "just a minute" that sent Adolf Hitler into a downward spiral, taking millions of innocent people with him. The cruelty and humiliation at age eleven that launched his drive for domination at any cost is completely understandable, even predictable, in retrospect.

Tragically, the lifelong impression that can set in motion a compassionate, caring, confident, productive member of society can just as quickly and easily be negative, inflicting a wound that festers and destroys a life—both in just a minute. It has broken my heart over these years of speaking as I have rounded the corner of my remarks and reluctantly pointed out the dark, shadowy side. I have so often seen an even quicker, more powerful response in the eyes before me. Suddenly many are transported back through time. They become that little child all over, being hurt, abused, and damaged. Their heads drop, tears well up in their eyes, they avert their gaze from me, staring off into the distance as they relive what happened. They still carry the sound of hurtful words ringing in their ears. They remember exactly where they were, how the room looked, even how it smelled. A clear and vivid memory of hurt and pain still haunts their lives.

But on the other hand, the power of a positive moment is sheer joy to recall. I was speaking to a conference of teachers in Nairobi, Kenya. They had allotted me an hour, but as usual, I needed only forty-five minutes. Teachers are very special, and I could see that many of those present were once again children in that moment, vividly remembering precious or painful moments of long ago.

So I paused and said, "Does this concept bring to mind a memory for anyone, perhaps a story that you are willing to share?"

A young man in the third row stood. He explained that he was now in his first year of teaching and absolutely loving it. He then told of his very troubled beginning as a first grader. He had a terrible stutter; he was timid and felt alone, even in a crowded classroom. He lived for recess and for dismissal at the end of the day. That is, until his homeroom teacher saw his struggle and stepped boldly into his world. She praised his work, wrote encouraging words on his papers, gave him some of the few hugs he ever received as a child.

He loved her and decided right then and there that he wanted to grow up to be a teacher, just like her. "So here I am, a grateful and enthusiastic teacher—all because of her." The audience clapped, assuming that was the end of his story.

"Did you ever tell her of her impact on your life?" I asked.

"No," he said softly, "I never really did."

"Do you think she even knows?" I pressed.

"Well, sir, she does now," he said as tears welled up in his eyes.

There was a hush across the crowd of perhaps 400 teachers. We were all imagining that the precious woman must have passed away, and he meant that she had perhaps heard his words from the balcony of heaven.

But then, when he had collected himself, he turned and pointed across the crowded room as he continued, ". . . because she is sitting right over there."

We all gasped and turned our heads to see where he was pointing. There sat an elderly, gray-haired woman. Her eyes were glistening, and amid the wild applause, she quietly stood to her feet, the perfectly poised teacher she had always been.

Now, I can't prove it, but I would swear violins were playing as the two of them made their way to the center aisle and met in a warm, lingering, long-overdue embrace.

I ended my message right there. "I'm done speaking," I announced. "I think you get it. That said it all!"

Through the powerful stories of others in this book, I hope you will take a moment and reflect on the influencers of your own childhood. Was it your mother? Your dad? Was it a teacher like for this young educator? Often, I've found it was a coach. Maybe your grandmother or grandpa? A pastor? A camp counselor? Another child maybe. A total stranger? By the end of the last chapter you will be convinced that any of us can wield a powerful effect, if we simply care and stay alert to the opportunity.

Section One

A MOMENT FOR RESCUE

My sportscaster friend Jerry Schemmel, now the well-known "Voice of the Colorado Rockies," survived the 1989 crash of United Flight 232 at Sioux City, Iowa. Miraculously he emerged safe in a cornfield, relieved and standing clear of the burning wreckage . . . when he heard a baby's screams still inside that smoke-filled fuselage. He dashed back into the carnage, followed the cries through the billowing smoke, and rescued a little eleven-month-old girl named Sabrina Michaelson. His story is told in his powerful book *Chosen to Live.*

As Jerry sat in my office reliving that story for me, I wanted to jump up and say, "Me too! That's what I would have done!"

But would I? Would you?

Nothing grips our hearts more on the evening news, putting a lump in our throats, than watching a firefighter rescue a shivering child from an icy lake—or a bloodied soldier hoisting his wounded friend onto his shoulder and carrying him to safety amid a hail of bullets and explosions. Such acts of selfless heroism cannot be rehearsed or anticipated. That amazing spirit either resides deep within us, or it doesn't. The drama seizes us in an unexpected moment, and we act—or we don't—in just a minute.

There are no second chances, no coulda-woulda-shoulda options. In the instant, heroes seldom know the full significance of what they are doing. In fact, they may never know. *Is this child's life a fair exchange for my own? If I die in the process of rescuing her, will she live to achieve more than I might have?* There is no time for such thoughts.

When, in retrospect, we learn years later what that child grew up to be, we say, "Wow, thank goodness!" But when we *don't* know, we should also say, "Wow, thank goodness!" A life is precious for what it *is,* not just for what it *does.* The truth is that every child is valuable. They are lovingly knit by their Creator in their mother's womb, one at a time. They are born one at a time. They live and die one at a time. And they can be rescued one at a time, usually by selfless heroes . . . notice, usually not by politicians, millionaires, or celebrities, but by ordinary people, with extraordinary hearts.

> In this crazy, fast-paced world, it is easy for the weakest, the most vulnerable, the littlest among us to get hurt in the stampede.

The Most Vulnerable

When the news cameras zoom back from the face of a specific boy or girl in peril to reveal the masses across our world, however, it is easy (and understandable) to move from empathy to apathy. The sheer magnitude of children in poverty is overwhelming. Most of society, even caring people, feel they can't possibly do all that needs to be done, and so they become paralyzed. They end up doing nothing. The great British statesman Edmund Burke is best remembered for this one sentence: "All that is necessary for the triumph of evil is for good people to do nothing."

In this crazy, fast-paced world, it is easy for the weakest, the most vulnerable, the littlest among us to get hurt in the stampede. They need our "just a minute" moment of safety and rescue that they so richly deserve.

That thought came to mind recently when I was driving along an Oregon highway. I came to a row of orange highway cones and flashing signs that said "Construction Zone. All fines doubled. Injure a worker and receive a $15,000 fine and mandatory jail time."

Needless to say, that got my attention. I slowed down and kept a wary eye out for the road crew. The last thing I wanted to do was to get that kind of fine . . . and, oh yes, to hurt a worker. Sadly, I believe it was in that order.

This warning was needed because in the everyday commutes of our lives, it is easy to miss the people and things going on around us. Yet these guys in a dangerous zone were concentrating on their construction work and needed the rest of us to watch out for them. They were vulnerable on that stretch of road.

As I cleared the area and sped off, I got to thinking. Isn't that exactly the mind-set we need to hold for the welfare of children in our world today? They are vulnerable to everything dangerous around them. They are concentrating on the busy task of growing up. They aren't yet aware of the hazards on all sides. Looking out for them should be our job.

If a child is around, we should be on high alert, not just to not harm them, but to rescue them when needed and to advance them lovingly in any way we can. Anything harmful done by society racing by should receive double the fine compared to causing the same harm to an adult! That might make criminals pause before robbing a store that has children in it, or breaking into a house where they see toys in the yard. "Oops, better watch out—there are children around here." It might slow down a pervert who is about to sexually molest a minor.

It is the duty of all of us who make up society to protect, nurture, and bless the children entrusted to us. Life, as we've said, has value because it *is*, not necessarily for what it *does*. But as a man named Herb Gilbey discovered, sometimes it's both.

ERRAND OF MERCY

WHEN THE SNOW IS FLYING and the wind is howling, you naturally want to stay inside your own warm home. Herb Gilbey certainly did that night back in 1918 as a blizzard roared across South Dakota. He wanted nothing more than to hold a cup of hot chocolate between his hands and look out the window.

But there was a knock at the door. His neighbor, a pharmacist, had come over for some reason. "Come in, come in—get out of the cold!" Herb said as he ushered his friend into the living room.

When the neighbor pulled back the scarf from his face, Herb could tell that he didn't look good. He knew the man had been working long hours, trying to help people all over town as they battled the flu epidemic that was in full force just then. They both had read in the papers that some 20 million Americans had been stricken so far, with thousands of deaths.

"Are you all right?" Herb inquired.

"Yes, I'll be okay," the man answered huskily. "But Pinky"—the nickname of his seven-year-old son—"has got it really bad. It's turned into pneumonia now. I don't know if he's going to make it. . . ." The father's voice cracked as he said this last sentence.

"Oh, no!" Herb replied. "Can we do anything to help?"

"Well . . . that's why I came over," the pharmacist replied. "There is a new drug—still kind of experimental—that seems to work pretty well against pneumonia. But I don't have any of it here. The closest place to get it is at the big supply house in Minneapolis. I was just wondering . . ." His voice trailed off.

Herb looked again at his neighbor's flushed face. The man was in no condition to attempt a drive of two hundred fifty miles east and then back again. What an ordeal that would be in this weather, even for a healthy person.

But . . . he couldn't just let little Pinky succumb. Herb thought for another moment, then said, "Okay. I'll give it a try. What's the address?"

Herb Gilbey went out and got his Model-T Ford started in the cold. It had no heater, but soon he was on the rough, mostly unpaved road anyway, headed for the Minnesota state line. He drove all night through the snowstorm, rarely topping thirty-five miles an hour. By morning, he arrived in the big city, found the supplier, got the medicine, and turned right around to start back to South Dakota.

Pinky survived.

Herb Gilbey passed away in due time, feeling gratified about his good deed for the neighbor boy. He didn't live long enough to see Pinky reach his full stature on the American stage . . . as a U.S. Senator and Vice President of the United States. People by then were calling him by his more proper name: Hubert H. Humphrey.

The child you rescue may hold incredible potential. A small act when the boy or girl is in jeopardy may change the course of history. We never know. Given that uncertainty, we always need to lean toward the side of protection and rescue.

The Humphrey story reminds me of a similar crisis that broke back in the early 1700s, when a cottage in Epworth, England, caught fire. The masterful biographer of John Wesley (known in childhood as "Jacky") opens his book this way:

PLUCKED FROM THE BURNING

THE ROOM SEEMED LIGHT already, yet the bed curtains were closed, and the nursemaid had not yet gotten him up. Jacky lay puzzled for a moment, then put out his head from the four-poster. He saw streaks of fire on the ceiling.

In the lurid glow he noticed that Molly and Anne, two of his sisters who slept in the same great bed with him, were gone, and the other bed, where the nurse slept with Patty and baby Charles, was empty. Five-year-old Jacky ran to the open door. The floor outside was ablaze. He ran back and climbed onto a chest of drawers near the window and pulled at the latch.

Above him the thatched roof of the rectory crackled and burned in the strong northeast wind. Below, a crowd of neighbors were gathered in the yard and were trying to douse the flames. Jacky edged onto the windowsill as far as he dared. He saw a man point up, then call out that he would fetch a ladder.

Another cried, "There will not be time!" This tall, burly neighbor leaned against the wall while eager hands helped a lighter man to climb onto his shoulders. As the heat behind Jacky grew intense, the fellow stood upright, stretched his arms, and plucked the boy out of the window. At that moment the roof fell in, "but it fell inward, or we had all been crushed at once."

They carried Jacky to the house where the family had taken refuge. Apparently Hetty, who was eleven, had been woken by a piece of burning thatch and had given the alarm. Their father, the rector of Epworth, had run to the room where his wife slept apart because she was ill and pregnant. She woke their eldest daughter, and they dashed through the flames to safety.

Then the rector rushed upstairs to the nursery. The maid seized baby Charles and ordered the others to follow, but no one noticed that Jacky lay fast asleep through the uproar. When the rector realized the child was missing, he tried to get up the stairs again, but they were on fire and would not bear his weight. In agony of mind he knelt in the hall and commended John Wesley's soul to God.

But here was Jacky safe and sound, "a brand plucked out of the burning."[1] The Reverend Samuel Wesley, his house in ashes, his books and writings gone, cried out in joy: "Come, neighbors! Let us kneel down! Let us give thanks to God! He has given me all eight children. Let the house go. I am rich enough!"[2]

Had that peasant not found the courage and strength to move close to the heat, becoming a human ladder to lift another up who would snatch a young lad from a burning window . . . well, the world might never have seen the great Methodist awakening that John Wesley spearheaded. No doubt that image led to the conversion of many listeners as he retold the story; they came to see themselves in the same danger as little Jacky, except for them it was the inferno of hell. And I assume that peasant surely got a shock when he entered heaven and discovered how many souls were present as a result of his "just a minute" moment.

Sometimes the rescue takes place before the child is even born. I have become convinced that the womb is in fact the most dangerous place on earth to be a child. Sometimes the risk is because of poverty. Sadly sometimes it is merely "inconvenience" that ends a life. In the following case, the endangered child has become a great hero of mine.

NOT AGAIN?

HIS PARENTS MARRIED during the Great Depression. Two children quickly arrived—and then, to their dismay, the young couple discovered they were pregnant with a third child before their fourth anniversary. Those were painfully tough financial times, and another child certainly wasn't in their plan.

But . . . against all logic they became convinced God had planned this child for them. They chose to have the baby, yet another one—this time a boy. And their son now writes, "I'm so grateful they did. . . . Our family came to know a joy in family life that we otherwise would never have known." Today, all three of those children are in Christian service. And as the noted preacher and author Chuck Swindoll says, "Because they thought those unselfish thoughts many years ago, I'm able to write these things today."[3]

This would come as no surprise to Chuck Swindoll, but if ever you wonder if God loves little children, notice His accounts of rescues in the nick of time. The Bible records at least three of them.

1. A priest's wife named Jehosheba, truly an unsung hero, snuck into the royal palace and snatched her infant nephew Joash away to safety. Otherwise his wicked grandmother, Queen Athaliah, would have killed him along with all his brothers. Seven years later, Joash was named king and went on to reign for four decades. Really—read it in 2 Kings 11.

2. We don't even know the name of the nurse who swept up Prince

Jonathan's little son Mephibosheth into her arms and fled as the royal house of King Saul was crashing to pieces all around him. In her haste, she tragically dropped the child, crippling him for life. But she *could* so easily in that panicked moment have saved her own neck and left him, just one more to be slaughtered. She didn't. Later as an adult, he was brought to the palace of King David to live the rest of his life in comfort, as a show of David's great love for Mephibosheth's father. This story appears in 2 Samuel 4:4 . . . you can't make this stuff up!

3. Finally, there's the great prophet Elijah, who in 1 Kings 17:17–23 wouldn't give up his vigil to bring back to life the dead son of a grieving widow who had been kind to him for a long time. Elijah, no newcomer to miracles, was disappointed that God didn't answer his fervent prayer. But he refused to stop praying for the boy, even though God didn't seem to be listening. He prayed not once, not twice, but three times, and would have prayed more if God had not then intervened and raised the boy to life. (I guess it sometimes takes more than "just a minute.")

Unknown but Not Forgotten

Sometimes the act of kindness we do for a child, though it takes just a minute, can reverberate for a lifetime. Like the ripples from a pebble tossed into a pond, we may never know how far our action spreads or where it finally comes to rest.

One of our Compassion International staff members in Colorado Springs has a wonderful teenage son. Christopher Dana was a model student, an athlete, and a godly young man. He had a minor curvature of his spine that required a fairly basic surgery to straighten things out as he was finishing up the development of his strong, growing body.

But something that morning in the operation went horribly wrong. In a matter of just minutes, Christopher was left paralyzed. Brokenhearted, I visited him in the hospital. *Oh, Lord, what do I possibly say to him?* I moaned as I entered the room.

I tried to say the right things that day, and then I prayed with him. Leaving, I wasn't sure I had been much help.

Months passed, and Christopher entered therapy. All of us at Compassion prayed daily for him and his overwhelmed family. In time I started hearing good reports from Sean and Michelle, his courageous parents.

One day, my assistant Angie came into my office, tears in her eyes. "I think you should come see this," she said quietly.

Out in the lobby sat Christopher in his wheelchair. As I approached him, he painfully stood to his feet! His father said, "Christopher has been working for many months with this one goal. He's wanted to come here and show you his ability to walk 200 feet—into your office." They had measured it off with tape on the floor.

I had rarely seen such courage. Step by step Christopher moved his feet, a smile on his face but at times contorted into a grimace of determination, all the way until he slowly eased himself down into the president's chair at my desk. We cheered wildly.

Then he pulled out a folded list of questions he had been drafting all these painful months.

"Dr. Stafford," he began, "who was the greatest influence on your life?"

My mind raced back to my precious father, a missionary in West Africa. I told Christopher how he had made me believe in myself. I described how we had built our house together on the hot, windswept plains . . . okay, I was just six years old and surely not much help, but he made me believe we had built it together! I told how he had managed to make his little son feel like a real partner in ministry, and how I, while away at boarding school, had worried that he couldn't possibly do his missionary work without me. "It was my dad, Christopher. He made me believe in myself."

We sat there in silence for a moment, lost in our thoughts. Then, on a whim, I asked him to answer the same question he had asked me.

"You, Mr. President," he replied. "When you visited me in my hospital room right after my injury, you told me, 'Christopher—never give up!'"

I could barely remember saying those words. The situation had been so grim, the odds so stacked against him. I had no idea the power of that sentence to motivate this young man. But in a single minute, my words had sunk into the cement of his soul, instilling him with courage and resolve beyond my wildest hope.

You never quite know when a young life is hanging by a thread.

Those few words, he told me, had carried him through the darkest nights, had convinced him to get up the next morning and keep trying. For months he had fallen and gotten up again—such pain, despair, determination—but also faith and courage. I'm sure many others must have said the same words in their visits. But so had I. And in such a minute, hope had found its way into the heart of this brave young man.

Little Jessica

You never quite know when a young life is hanging by a thread, physically or otherwise, and your intervention will make a major difference. You don't know the significance of the moment. I've seen it happen time and again.

One of my most precious Compassion moments was on the far side of the world, in Manado, Indonesia. The little church I entered that day was constructed of weather-beaten, hand-hewn wood from the surrounding jungle. The 100 or so children had gathered in the sanctuary and were all sitting cross-legged on the wood floor, their eyes eager to see these strange visitors who had arrived. Their teachers stood along the walls; mothers and a few fathers gathered shyly at the back of the room.

The children sang and danced and recited Scripture and poetry for us. So poor, yet so precious in every way. Then I was asked if I wanted to say a few words to them.

I thought fast. What could I say to let them know how precious they were, how loved by Compassion, by their little church . . . as well as their sponsors on the other side of the world? I started in a lighthearted vein: "In all the world I have never seen a place with such beautiful children!" I exclaimed. "Your parents must be so very proud of you! You produce such lovely singing. And all those Bible verses! You must be very, very smart."

The children giggled. The teachers were smiling, eyes twinkling with gratitude. The poverty-stricken parents looked at their little ones with newfound respect and pride.

"Does anybody know what you want to be when you grow up?" I asked. A few brave hands went up.

"A soldier," one boy said.

"A policeman," said another.

"A teacher," added a third. The adults beamed.

"A pastor," said a fourth.

I pointed out a little boy and said, "I think I see a future doctor." He grinned. "And look!" I continued. "Somewhere in this room might be a future President of Indonesia! Do you know which one? No? Well, you'd better treat every child here like you would the President of your country, because you never know!" The room buzzed with excitement.

In the very front row, sitting at my feet, was a beautiful but frail little girl, maybe six years old. Her eyes were looking up at me wide in wonder. She was too shy to have shouted out any dreams.

My heart paused a moment. I had an idea.

"Do you know how precious you all are to God? He knows you and loves you more than anything else in the whole world. Like this little girl . . ." I knelt down and gently lifted her up in my arms. "Do any of you know her name?"

"Jessica," they all called out. I looked at her face, and she shyly nodded; they had it right.

"Jesus knows Jessica's name," I said. "But do any of you know how many hairs she has on her head?" Silence.

"Jesus does! He loves little Jessica so much that He keeps track of everything about her, even the number of hairs on her head.

"Did you ever look closely at the tips of your fingers? See those tiny lines, that little design? Jesus made every one of you unique, special." I took Jessica's little fingers in my hands. "God loved Jessica so much he drew her very own picture on her fingers like nobody else's in the whole world." Jessica looked intently at her fingers, until a shy smile formed. She snuggled deeper into my arms.

"God knew her before she was even born. He knit her in her mama's womb. And look—he made her beautiful, gave her her very own laugh, her beautiful eyes. He knows exactly what she will be when she grows up. She has no idea how special she is to God, and how loved. Jesus would have died on the cross for her even if she was the only child on earth!"

The room grew suddenly quiet. As I glanced around at the teachers, I saw eyes brimming. A tear trickled down the craggy face of the peasant pastor beside me. Something seemed to be happening here. . . .

I laid my hand on little Jessica's head and prayed. I thanked God for every child in that church, but especially for Jessica's life and for loving her so much. Then I moved to place her back on the floor where I'd found her.

But her arms held tightly around my neck. Slowly, reluctantly, she released me. In her eyes I saw tears like those of the teachers'. What was going on here? What had turned the party atmosphere into a somber moment?

I returned to my chair to sit down. A few minutes later, the pastor leaned over to whisper, "You couldn't possibly have known—but if ever a little girl needed to be lovingly held and affirmed, it was Jessica right now."

Why was that? Before leaving that place, the staff told me with broken hearts that just a month or so earlier, little Jessica had been savagely raped by a man in her neighborhood. She had been so violated that she needed surgery, stitches, and hospitalization. The pastor and the church had courageously pressured the legal authorities on her behalf. But the man had gotten off with no penalty, no jail, nothing—by paying a bribe of just $300.

The little church was devastated. Once again in poverty, justice had failed, and the poor had paid the price. An innocent little girl had suffered the brutality of a world that has lost its heart. "We are amazed that she would even let you, a man, pick her up and hold her in your arms," the teachers said.

Years have passed since that incident, and I'm told that our brief moment together was the beginning of her healing. She is beginning to blossom again in mind, soul, and spirit.

I carry a picture of Jessica with me now. I am so grateful that I got to be a part of a "moment" that is healing and transforming her life day by day.

* * * * * *

So, do mere minutes matter? Can God use any of us to be that moment's hero? Can a minute transform a life? Can a child be snatched from death's door? Can a minute of loving words breathe a lifetime of newfound hope in the darkest of hours? Can a single act of kindness ripple on for eternity, blessing others we may never meet or know?

The answer is yes . . . oh, yes! Deep within the spirit of all of us resides an amazing hero just waiting for the moment, for the curtains of life to open so we can walk out onto the stage and do the right thing that will make all the difference.

Section Two

A MOMENT TO BUILD SELF-WORTH

The rescue of a child in physical danger or other visible peril is noble, to be sure. But not all needs present themselves so dramatically.

I happen to believe that children carry with them at all times a little invisible chalkboard, a blank slate that they hold up to us saying essentially, "Please tell me something. Something about myself. Something about my life, my world." As we'll see in the stories of this section, the words we then speak or the actions we take at that pivotal moment can change the trajectory of a little life from that moment forward.

Of course, we sometimes miss their silent pleas for affirmation. We're not quite alert to what they are thinking and wondering about themselves. We need to step in and actually create the interaction, believing that whenever a child comes into our field of vision, it has the potential to be a divine appointment. God has ordained for two paths to cross—ours and the child's.

These are some of my favorite, most powerful stories. They show the incredible value of a heart tuned in to lifting up a child. Not all of them are hugely life-changing. Some are just the account of how a "minute" of insight and kindness got a child through a frustrating or exhausting event. Like this one, for example . . .

Look at Those Shoes!

It was Easter weekend, and Denver International Airport was a boiling river of humanity all scrambling to get somewhere in a hurry. I, too, was dashing off in too big a rush to shine my shoes. I climbed into a shoeshine chair in Concourse B, the nerve center of United Air Lines. From my elevated perch I had a pretty good vantage point to see the madness around me.

I had stopped at this stand enough times in the past to know these guys and enjoy their easy banter, teasing each other and commenting on the news. I also knew how instinctively they noticed the shoes all around them. "We hate summer!" they'd told me. "Everybody wears sneakers and sandals—now how you gonna make any money with that goin' on?"

On this day we watched as a harried young mom came struggling, upstream, toward us. She had a very reluctant four-year-old son in tow. They both looked exhausted and exasperated. He was dragging his feet, holding back as they navigated the concourse. In fact, he looked a lot like a water-skier behind his mom, the towboat.

When they reached us, it all collapsed. The little boy completely stopped, unable to muster one more step. His mother's purse kept falling off her shoulder as she tightened her motherly grip on his little fingers and pleaded, "Come on! We're almost there." At a dead standstill right at my feet, she blew a wisp of hair off her forehead and glared at her son, dejected. The little boy was wearing sneakers that had flashed blue and red lights along the edges as he had shuffled along. But by now, believe me, the lights were out.

Just at that moment, A.J. the shoeshine man spoke up. "Mm, mm, mm," he chanted, with a wry smile on his face. "Would you look at that boy's shoes! What are those?" The weary lad looked down at his shoes and then up at A.J.

The guy shining my shoes paused, turned around, and quickly picked up the trail. "I sure do wish I had me a pair of shoes like that!"

The exhausted mother and son now both looked up blankly, surprised that anyone in the crowded terminal had noticed them. The mother gave a weak smile.

Just then, the third shoe shiner, a woman, chimed in. "You boys know what those are, don'cha?" she said with a twinkle in her eye. "Those are *marchin'* shoes! You should see how those shoes can *march!*"

The little boy looked down at his shoes like he had never seen them before. Then suddenly he straightened his back, squared his little shoulders, smiled, and took off high-stepping down the concourse with all the aplomb of the Queen's Guard at Buckingham Palace. *Step! Step! Step!* His astonished mother was pulled into his wake; now *she* was the waterskier. Off they strode toward the awaiting gate.

But just before they melded into the crowd, the mother looked back, purse halfway down her arm, to mouth the words, *"Thank you! Thank you! Thank you!"* her face flushed with amazement. At the shoe stand, it was all cheers and high fives. The drama had unfolded in less than a minute.

It doesn't take much time to let a child know he can make it after all, that hope can jump-start the soul. That moment probably didn't change his entire life—maybe he wouldn't even remember it tomorrow—but it had gotten him and his grateful mom through a very difficult, frustrating moment.

The Kindness of Strangers

Those shoeshine heroes didn't know that lad and probably would never see him again. That really doesn't matter. The truth is, sometimes the voice or action of a complete stranger breaks through the normal run of things and boosts children into a whole new perspective. Like this . . .

THE WAVE GAME

I WAS DRIVING HOME from running some errands and was behind a large SUV filled with what appeared to be a family of three young boys and their parents on an outing.

This brought back memories of trips my family used to take, with my mother behind the wheel of the station wagon. We would all be loaded up with snacks and other neat stuff. "Are we there yet?" we would keep asking; you know how that goes. These were some of the best times growing up.

All three of the youngsters ahead of me today were facing my car, just staring. I thought about how my brothers, sister and I used to try to get people to wave from any of the other cars around us. Most of the time, they were too busy driving to wave back. We got mostly frowns and brief nods. When someone actually did wave, we would shriek with laughter and wave frantically back.

I suddenly got an urge to wave at the children in front of me. They simultaneously smiled and waved back. This made me smile. They would turn to their parents momentarily as if to tell them of our communication. We continued waving at each other. This moment was wonderful. I couldn't help but giggle.

We kept this up for a few more minutes, until I decided to pass this family and head on my way. I smiled again as I waved good-bye from the left lane.

However . . . this was not to be the last of our contact. We ended up getting off the highway at the same exit. The father now motioned to pull me over. Instinctively, I got nervous; my mother had always taught me to be cautious about strangers. But I knew we were close to the tollbooths, so I felt safe in stopping.

The father got out and walked over to my car. I rolled down my window to see a wide-smiling face. "My name is Bill," he said. "I'm on a trip across the country with my sister and my three sons. My wife recently passed away, and my boys are quite uneasy about the trip. I want to thank you for what you did."

I told him I wasn't quite sure what he was thanking me for.

"My boys had been miserable this entire trip until you waved at them. You should know that you made a difference in their lives, even if it is just for a brief moment. I want to thank you for being so kind."

I smiled as I said, "I lost my mother three years ago. You and your boys brought back fond memories for me. Thank *you* for reminding me of great times our family spent on the road while I was growing up. You and your boys have made *my* day a little brighter, also."

I wished him well and said good-bye. I drove alongside his

vehicle as he returned to it. I gave one final wave to the boys as I passed. All three smiled and waved back.

In the beginning, right after my mother died, I thought I would never get through the grief I felt. I cried every time I thought of her. Now, I tend to smile at her memory. I've decided never to get too busy driving to wave.[4]

—MISTY L. KERL

Kindness—from Across the World

Whether delivered face-to-face on the church steps or through a long-distance call or piece of mail, the message of kindness is potent. At Compassion International, we repeatedly tell our sponsors that their most valuable gift to the child with whom they are linked is not the monthly check that supports their education and health care. It's their prayers and words of encouragement through letters from a world away.

If you have read *Too Small to Ignore,* you know I grew up in a poverty-stricken West African village where over half of my childhood friends died before I was fifteen years old. **I know poverty. I hate poverty. I hate what it does to little children.** Its worst aspects, however, are not the lack of clean water or sanitation or housing. It's not even the lack of money. Those things, tragic as they are, are not poverty. They are just the symptoms that dominate life when poverty is around.

Yes, it's good to attack the externals and eliminate them. But I know from my childhood, my academic studies, and now decades of serving the poor that the real root of poverty lies well beneath these visible conditions. It's the message it breathes into the heart of even very little children: *Give up. Nobody cares about you. Nothing will ever change. You are nothing and always will be.*

> **What we at Compassion do is rush to those dying embers before the glow is gone completely.**

Oh, the surrounding circumstances contribute to that worldview, to be sure. But when that hopeless life message finds root in a child's heart (and it can happen very early in life), the spirit of the child begins to shrivel. It wilts like a flower in the heat. The eyes grow downcast; the twinkle is gone. The fire begins to go out.

What we at Compassion do is rush to those dying embers before the glow is gone completely. With the local church, our staff, and sponsors at a distance, we frantically fan those embers until a *poof* of flame bursts forth. It's a beautiful thing to see. I fight tears even now as I describe it. You see, something has to reverse the downward spiral. There has to be an infusion of love and hope, often from outside one's immediate setting. In my doctoral studies at Michigan State University I documented the incredible impact of a loving, hopeful voice . . . the voice of kindness.

That is what lodged in the soul of Michelle Tolentino, a former Compassion child whom I love like my own daughters. Here is her story:

UP FROM DESPAIR

I WAS BORN in a squatters' area of Manila, one of the most congested places you can imagine. With both of my parents jobless, and two younger brothers to provide for, our family could not even afford our own shack. We had to live with relatives—seventeen of us staying in a very small shanty.

Food was scarce for us. My mom was forced to beg for food from friends and relatives. Every day outside our shack there would be lots of violence, neighbors fighting in the street. Shirtless men sat drinking alcohol all day, while bored women gambled, oblivious of their naked little children running around and playing in the filthy canals full of raw sewage.

But even worse in that slum was the rampant drug abuse. Like many others, my father was a drug addict himself. Even as a young girl, I knew that my life was hopeless, my future uncertain. I loved my father and thought he was a good man. But one of my earliest memories was waking up one morning to a lot of yelling and fighting inside our house. Some people said he stole from them in order to buy drugs. My world was shattered as my father was thrown out.

Life only got worse after that. In this pressure cooker of poverty and overcrowding, words flew that were far from kind. I felt so worthless, so vulnerable, that I was nothing and had no future.

The first glimmer of hope came at age five, when my aunt brought me to Calvary Foursquare Church, which had a Compassion Project. From the moment I stepped inside, I knew my life would change. The first thing they taught me in that place was that Jesus loved me. It was a simple but life-changing thought that would affect my whole destiny.

I learned how to pray, to talk to God. I read the Bible. My first-ever Bible was given to me by my Compassion sponsor. It was very precious to me, because I learned through the Scriptures that God was my Father, and I was His precious child. He was a Father to fatherless children like me.

I also felt that great love of my heavenly Father through my loving sponsors' letters from a world away. Their letters gave me so much encouragement. I remember in the winter of 1995 that they sent me a picture of themselves sitting on a park bench surrounded by snow. I had never seen such a sight. They sent me letters telling me, "Our dear Michelle, you are very beautiful in our eyes. You are very precious to us. We love you. We are praying for you."

Their words touched the very depth of my heart and soul. God used them in healing my broken self-image and destroyed self-worth. Every time I received their letters, I knew I was loved, I was important, and I was valued. I had a bright future ahead of me in the hands of my loving heavenly Father, who said in Jeremiah 29:11, "I know the plans I have for you, says the Lord, plans to prosper you and not to harm you, plans to give you hope and a future."

Michelle did indeed have a future. She blossomed, pursued her dreams, and eventually completed a degree in communication arts from the best university in the Philippines. She then earned a master's degree from Moody Theological Seminary in Chicago, graduating *summa cum laude*. She is now a traveling speaker on behalf of children and women at risk.

She is also "paying it forward" in other ways, sponsoring her own little child, Andrew, from the Philippine island of Samar. She says, "My prayer for Andrew is that he will know in his heart that Jesus loves him, and that someday, when God calls him to build a family, that he will be a loving father to his children."

She tells her story joyfully now and always includes this line: "I remember Papa Wess telling me, 'Michelle, you may have been born in poverty, but poverty was not born in you!'"

This is just one of more than two million children worldwide who have graduated from Compassion's sponsorship over the past sixty years. They've all discovered, in one way or another, the amazing power of love.

An Unlikely Source

But that love has to have a source from somewhere. For some sponsors, it springs from a painful memory of their own:

"ONLY" A GIRL

I WAS SITTING on the back patio with my dad reading a magazine when the truth finally came out. He was a naval officer—our family had lived everywhere from London to Florida to the Midwest—and I was his only child. My parents had tried to conceive for three years following marriage and had pretty much given up, choosing then to try for adoption—when suddenly I came along. At that time it was nearly impossible to adopt after having one biological child.

Now I was a young teenager. "Hey, Dad—it says here that they did a poll of parents," I said as the warm sun beat down upon our heads, "asking if they would choose to have kids again. And the majority said 'No!'"

My father looked up, turned toward me, and then made two straightforward statements: "Oh—well, we certainly wanted to have children. But we'd rather have had a boy." And with that, he went back to his own reading.

I sucked in my breath. To hear him bluntly say how he truly felt was a stab in my heart. I wasn't totally surprised, though; he'd just never quite said it this overtly before. I knew better than to start a debate with him; we never really delved into things together. And I certainly wasn't going to show any emotion, which would have backfired terribly. I could only silently get up and go back inside the house.

My dad was from an old-school upbringing, one of two sons of a very autocratic father. His name was a "Jr.," and my mother had once told me that if I had been a boy, I would have been a "III." Being a military officer, Dad was used to giving orders and having them promptly carried out. The gender of his child, however, was the one thing beyond his command. Now there was no one to carry on the family name—a disappointment to him, for sure.

Should I tell my mother about the patio exchange? No. There was no reason to upset her; after all, she had her own "moments" with my father. But on the inside, it hurt me deeply. It also made me angry. In fact, it birthed within me a determination to seek equality, to do whatever I could to change the world's assumption that boys are better.

After I finished growing up and got married, our first child was a boy. But the next two were girls. My husband and I raised them all to value both male and female, to appreciate the contributions of each. I read them stories with girl heroes as well as boy heroes. We took them to special museums that highlighted the achievements of notable women as well as men.

Today our family sponsors a total of eleven Compassion children, spread from Thailand to Central America, from Africa to Indonesia— *all girls.* It's my way of continuing the mission that started back on that day when I was in middle school. I want these girls to grow up to make a difference in their societies, some of which are even more tradition-bound than mine. When I write to them, I make sure they know that God created them as young women for a purpose—which should never be a source of dishonor but rather of courage and confidence.

This woman lives in an eastern state and has been a Girl Scout leader for more than a decade. Her older two children are now in college; the third is finishing high school. Her "just a minute" experience was painful and negative, to be sure. But it has been turned to wonderfully positive outcomes.

Full Circle

Sometimes, and in very unique circumstances, I've had the great privilege to see these powerful "just a minute" moments come full circle—when the one who has been inspired and encouraged turns into the encourager of someone else.

A few years ago I was visiting Compassion's work in Bolivia. One of our sponsored children named Jenny had not only graduated from our normal program but had been selected for our Leadership Development Program—a very select group sent on to university. They participate in an intense program to fully develop their potential and leadership ability.

It was graduation time, and Jenny's sponsors had traveled all the way from Oregon to honor and celebrate her achievement. Jenny came from a very poor family who lived way up in the high altitude of the Andes Mountains overlooking La Paz. The La Paz airport is so high (13,325 feet) that pilots don't even slow down to land in that rarified air, for fear of losing lift. They come screaming in to touch down at nearly full throttle; the runway goes on for two and a half miles. No wonder the airport is called *El Alto* ("The Heights").

Up on this *Altiplano* is where some of Bolivia's poorest people live. It had always been Jenny's dream to be a nurse—but of course, that would be a real stretch. After all, her father fixed bicycles for a living. She studied hard as a child, however, and managed to get accepted into La Paz University's School of Nursing. Moving away from her little adobe home high up in the mountains to live in the big city was scary. The academics were daunting. When she wrote to her sponsors pleading for their prayer support, their replies always carried the same message: "We are so very proud of you, Jenny. You can do this. Look how far you've come. Sweetheart, don't give up . . . do your best."

Jenny had listened and worked diligently. Not only had she just now graduated as a full-fledged nurse; she had graduated number one in her class! She had competed with the children of Bolivia's elite and powerful families and had come out on top. Her sponsors were so proud of her as she took us on a tour of the nursing school. She was obviously loved and respected by teachers and everyone we met.

Then we made the arduous trip up the mountain to her little home. It was simple, but immaculate, showing the dignity and pride of her parents. She then offered to take us to the Compassion project where she had been nurtured. It was a jostling two-mile jeep ride, a journey she had made on foot every day of her childhood.

When we arrived at the little mud church, nobody was expecting our visit. All of the children happened to be in the simple sanctuary for a group meeting just then. As Jenny and three very strange-looking white people walked in together, the peasant pastor looked up, surprised. Then recognizing his former student in her pristine white nurse's uniform, he remembered her love for the guitar and her lovely voice.

"Welcome back, Jenny!" he cried. "Come, please sing a song for the children." At the urging of the children she quietly walked to the front of the little church and took the old guitar from her pastor.

The children, about a hundred of them, were sitting on narrow rough-hewn benches, pressed tightly together. *Like chickens on a roost,* I thought to myself. They were so cute. Everything was brown—the floor, the walls, the children, and even their clothes—except for Jenny's uniform. The children cheered in excitement.

She sat down at the front of the church, tuned the guitar, and then began singing sweetly. About halfway through her song, I noticed she began looking, her eyes fixed, at just one place. Then I saw a tear trickle down her beautiful Spanish face. In a minute, I could see the object of her gaze: a little girl at the end of the third row. The girl was so small that her feet were swinging above the dirt floor.

Suddenly Jenny's voice cracked. Tears filled her eyes, and she stopped singing.

"Sweetheart," I heard her say softly to the little girl, "that is where I used to sit when I was little like you. You are sitting in my place. Do you see what has happened to me? That can happen to you—don't ever, ever give up!"

At that moment, Jenny looked up and across to the back of the church. I watched as her eyes met the eyes of her sponsors from Oregon. That's all I saw, because just then . . . well, everything went blurry for me.

I love it that so many of Compassion's worldwide sponsors have discovered that, while it is true that just a "minute" can transform a little life that is standing right in front of you, the same is absolutely true for just a "sentence" in a letter to a child half a world away. We saw this in Michelle's life and now again in Jenny's story. If you are linked to a child through Compassion or any other sponsorship organization, I urge you to seize the moment to sit down today and write a letter that lifts up your child. Look for anything in their past letters or reports that you can praise. Look for any signs of hurt or discouragement that you can counter with a word of encouragement. Look for any success that you can highlight and cheer with them. These, even brief notes, can be a lifeline of hope that reaches straight into their little hearts.

Whenever I visit Compassion children in their jungle huts, slum shanties, or country cottages, I am quick to ask if their sponsors have written them letters. I usually get a huge smile, followed by a scamper to a secret hideaway in a back corner of the room, from which they return joyfully clutching a plastic baggie in their tiny hands. These are the treasured letters and pictures from their sponsor—a beloved relationship on the other side of the world. Words have life-giving power. I urge you to send them!

Kindness—from the Heart of a Teacher

When we think about who we "owe" for our present quality of life, we quickly realize our deep debt to the teachers who have touched our lives. Beyond the actual subject matter of whatever class they taught us, they instilled in us important lessons about life, values, discipline, and effort and its rewards. With their lives, even more than their words, they gave us a passion to learn and modeled a generous, selfless life. (Okay, not all of them, now that I think of it! But most, to be sure.)

It's actually ridiculous the shabby way we pay teachers in our society compared to the money and privilege we throw at achievers in other fields of endeavor. Can you imagine giving a guided tour to a visitor from another planet, say, Mars? If asked to explain our priorities here on Earth, you might say, "Oh yes, we value our future and those in whose hands it is formed. Preparing the next generation to take its place, add value, and make it even better . . . well, nothing is more important.

"Oh, but look—there goes a basketball star! Excuse me, I'm going to go try to get his autograph. This guy is really tall and can throw a ball through that little hoop over there. We love that! And so we give him a ton of money to do it. We will give him as much money for each evening's game as we pay teachers for their whole year's effort . . . You say you don't understand? Is there a problem?"

As crazy as that sounds, it is absolutely true. And to their credit, most teachers follow their hearts, not their heads, into teaching. They don't do this for the pay. But over the years, whenever I have asked people about their most powerful "just a minute" experiences, teachers have consistently emerged as the greatest heroes among us.

For example, Tali Whiteley tells about her high school days, trying to transfer mid-year to Jacksonville, Florida's, Douglas Anderson School of the Arts to escape the horror of a sexual attack at her previous school. Her father, a rabbi, was initially told that enrollment in the new school was impossible. The anxious teenager listened through the wall to the conversation with the principal. . . .

THE GREEN JOURNAL

"RABBI, I UNDERSTAND your position, but we only hold auditions in the summer." For the first time in my life, I heard my father weep. I pressed my head tight against the great door, felt the cold on my cheek, and closed my eyes.

My father's voice interrupted. "She was raped by a group of boys at her school a month ago. She can't go back there."

I auditioned for The School of the Arts that day, sitting at the piano in the stuffy little practice room. . . . I laid my hands heavily on the yellow-stained keys and with my heart, with tears, with pain, I played Rachmaninoff, Beethoven, and finally, my father's favorite Chopin *Nocturne.* The teacher nodded, the principal put her hand up to her mouth and shook her head, and my father's face melted into quiet relief.

It wasn't until Friday, however, that I met Mrs. Jones, when I transferred into her creative writing class at 11:00 a.m. She always seemed to wear brown sandals, a blue flower-printed skirt, and a wrinkled white blouse with its frilly collar bent. She held a constant confused expression and played with a charm on her necklace. As she walked closer to my desk in the corner, I noticed she was pigeon-toed. She didn't bend over me the way other teachers had, but rather knelt at my desk, and smiled at me, eye-level.

"We'll be working in our journals today," Mrs. Jones said softly. She smelled like soap and mothballs and lilacs. "Do you have a notebook you can use as your journal?"

I could feel the inquisitive eyes in the classroom on "the new girl." A pretty blonde in the front of the room mumbled loudly to her neighbor about my "special audition."

"Get to work, please," Mrs. Jones told the class. *Please,* I thought. I believe it was the first time I had ever heard a teacher say "please" to a student.

I pulled a green notebook out of my book bag, and Mrs. Jones laid her cool, dry hand on mine. "I'm so happy to have you in my class," she whispered.

That journal, I now believe, saved me from insanity. I wrote every-thing that day and from that day forward; I turned myself inside out and dumped it into my green notebook the way I'd seen my mother plop her matzo balls into her chicken soup. I wrote about "them." I wrote their names down and crossed them out, then wrote them again and again, until it didn't hurt so much to hear them in my head. I wrote the word *rape* in red because it felt hot and burned and it was sore and I knew that even if I ignored it, it would not go away.

Mrs. Jones didn't judge my words the way the district attorney had. She didn't probe and pry and prick me like the psychologists or the nurse examiner at the hospital. She didn't insult and blame and scream like my mother initially had—or weep like my father. Mrs. Jones became much more than my English teacher. She was a partner in my internal battle, guiding me with her red-penned words on the many pages of my always-read, always-understood journal.[5]

No wonder that after finishing college, Tali Whiteley chose to become an English teacher.

The Still Small Voice of Mothers

The words of a loving mom can register powerfully at times . . . if we're paying attention, that is. Of course, that voice sometimes gets lost in the din of life. I admit there were occasions when my mother would insist she had told me six times to pick my clothes up off the floor, and I honestly hadn't heard her even once. (That's my story, and I'm stickin' to it!) Did her voice broadcast on some sort of high frequency that my inner short-wave radio just couldn't receive? What a mystery.

At other times, I did hear her voice but filtered it through a screening. She would call me to come inside the house, and from a hundred yards away I could discern the level of urgency and response required of me—or not. There was a world of difference between the first call of "Wess, come on in" in sort of a gentle, singsong way and the final life-or-death threat call I held out for. The first call signified, *No big deal. Just play on.* The second one, five minutes later, had a slight edge to it, as the "Wess" part was composed of three distinct notes, with an imaginary exclamation point at the end. The final one could not be ignored, thanks to its additional line of "Get in here *now*—I mean it!" or in extreme cases, "Don't make me get your father!"

Quit snickering . . . you've been there, too.

But it is an altogether different story when we're afraid, when the task looms too large, when someone has hurt our feelings. In these moments, we crave the words of a loving mother. We need an ally, a defender, a shelter in life's storm. Often throughout the growing-up years, we need someone to believe in us when few others do. We seek for someone who will always be on our side.

Here's one example:

FERVENT FAN

RON WAS FIFTEEN years old, a tenth-grade student, the only sophomore suiting up on game day with the varsity team. Excitedly, he invited his mother to attend. It was her very first football game, and she promised to be there with several friends.

The game finally ended. She waited outside the locker room to drive Ron home.

"What did you think of the game, Mom? Did you see the three touchdown passes our team made? Did you see our tough defense? How about the fumble on the kickoff return that we recovered?"

She replied, "Ron, you were magnificent. You have such presence, and I noticed the pride you took in the way you looked. You pulled up your knee socks eleven times during the game, and I could tell you were perspiring under all those bulky pads, because you got eight drinks and splashed water on your face twice. I really like how you went out of your way to pat Number Nineteen, Number Five, and Number Ninety on the back every time they came off the field."

Ron was stumped. "Mom, how did you know all that? And how can you say I was magnificent? I didn't even get to play in the game."

His mother smiled and answered, "Ron, I don't know anything about football. I didn't come here to watch the game. I came to watch you!"[6]

—DAN CLARK

Sometimes a mother's reinforcement is more indirect. But once we realize what is going on, we value it all the more, as Marsha Arons explains in this true account.

THE WHITE GARDENIA

EVERY YEAR on my birthday, from the time I turned twelve, one white gardenia was delivered anonymously to me at my house. There was never a card or note, and calls to the florist were in vain because the purchase was always made in cash. After a while, I stopped trying to discover the identity of the sender. I just delighted in the beauty and heady perfume of that one magical, perfect white flower nestled in folds of soft pink tissue paper.

But I never stopped imagining who the sender might be. Some of my happiest moments were spent in daydreams about someone wonderful and exciting, but too shy or eccentric to make known his or her identity. In my teen years it was fun to speculate that the sender might be a boy I had a crush on, or even someone I didn't know who had noticed me.

My mother often contributed to my speculations. She'd ask me if there was someone for whom I had done a special kindness, who might be showing appreciation anonymously. She reminded me of the times when I'd been riding my bike and our neighbor drove up with her car full of groceries and children. I always helped her unload the car and made sure the children didn't run into the road. Or maybe the mystery sender was the old man across the street. I often retrieved his mail during the winter, so he wouldn't have to venture down his icy steps.

My mother did her best to foster my imagination about the gardenia. She wanted her children to be creative. She also wanted us to feel cherished and loved, not just by her, but by the world at large.

When I was seventeen, a boy broke my heart. The night he called for the last time, I cried myself to sleep. When I awoke in the morning, there was a message scribbled on my mirror in red lipstick: "Heartily know, when half-gods go, the gods arrive." I thought about that quotation from Emerson for a long time, and I left it where my mother had written it until my heart healed. When I finally went for the glass cleaner, my mother knew that everything was all right again.

But there were some hurts my mother couldn't heal. A month before my high school graduation, my father died suddenly of a heart attack. My feelings ranged from simple grief to abandonment, fear, distrust, and overwhelming anger that my dad was missing some of the most important events of my life. I became completely uninterested in my upcoming graduation, the senior class play, and the prom—events I had worked on and looked forward to. I even considered staying home to attend college instead of going away as I had planned, because it felt safer.

My mother, in the midst of her own grief, wouldn't hear of me missing out on any of these things. The day before my father died, she and I had gone shopping for a prom dress and had found a spectacular one—yards and yards of dotted Swiss in red, white, and blue. Wearing it made me feel like Scarlett O'Hara. But it was the wrong size, and when my father died the next day, I forgot all about the dress.

My mother didn't. The day before the prom, I found that dress waiting for me—in the right size. It was draped majestically over the living room sofa, presented to me artistically and lovingly. I may not have cared about having a new dress, but my mother did.

She cared how we children felt about ourselves. She imbued us with a sense of the magic in the world, and she gave us the ability to see beauty even in the face of adversity. In truth, my mother wanted her children to see themselves much like the gardenia—lovely, strong, perfect, with an aura of magic and perhaps a bit of mystery.

My mother died when I was twenty-two, only ten days after I was married. That was the year the gardenias stopped coming.[7]

It is one of life's sad mysteries that the more we love and are loved, the more painful is our loss when it ceases. Sometimes love comes in the form of mere moments delivered "just in time." But as we've just seen, sometimes we are blessed enough to be the recipient of a tapestry of memories lovingly and deliberately woven together over the years. If you find yourself in the midst of such a thoughtful relationship, treasure it! Rejoice, be grateful, give back, and pass it on. You have been uncommonly blessed.

When mothers—like the white-gardenia mom—get it right, they're often really, really right. But parenting is hard work. Children are not born with an instruction manual clutched in their tiny hands. Sometimes we don't always say or do the right thing on their behalf. Sometimes we don't know any better; sometimes we are just too exhausted or perhaps too hurt ourselves to have anything left to give to our children . . . even in just a minute.

That's where God's grace, the kindness of others, or the sheer strength of the human character is forced to step in.

APPLE OF HER EYE

THE PASTOR'S HOME where I grew up back in the 1950s, in Oshawa, Ontario, was a place that emphasized diligence and responsibility. To praise a child—what we now call affirmation—would be to build evil pride and create a "big head," it was believed. You didn't get told you had done a good job; it was just expected.

I came running home from school one day when I was about eight years old with a piece of plaster art I had painted—two apples with three leaves on top, and a wire hanger on the back. It certainly was no masterpiece, but I was happy with it. "Mother, look what I made!" I exclaimed.

Her only reply was, "Yes, well, put it in the living room." A bit crestfallen, I trudged away to place it on the coffee table.

Later that day, a woman from our congregation stopped by to visit my mother. I knew the rules: If the French doors were closed, it meant we children were to occupy ourselves elsewhere during the visit. If the doors were open, we were allowed to participate.

The doors were open just then, so I came in to where the two women sat. I said hello to the visitor.

Soon she asked with a bright face, "Did you paint this, Ruth?"

"Yes," I shyly answered.

"Well, I'm very impressed!" she said. Turning to my mother, she continued, "Isn't it lovely, Olive?"

My mother was trapped. What could she do but agree? "Yes, it's very nice," she said.

A warm feeling swelled up in my heart. I'd never heard that kind of compliment before. Some adult actually thought I had done a good job.

I can't claim that the incident made a change in my mother's view of affirmation, although it did seem that as my siblings and I reached the teen years, she was less critical than before. Neither can I claim to have developed into a great artist, although I did take some art classes in high school and enjoyed them.

The greatest effect on me, especially as I became a wife and mother myself, was to cement the importance of building up a child's esteem and encouraging them in whatever good things they attempt. My husband had to remind me from time to time, especially in the early years, because I wasn't in the habit. But I soon caught on.

And I must also report that with the passing years, my mother has come to do the same. She freely heaps praise on the heads of her grandchildren. We've all learned a valuable lesson.

—RUTH RATZ

Jennifer Peters is my friend. She is one of the kindest, most affirming people I know. She honed her skills as an international flight attendant with Northwest Airlines. Keeping passengers smiling all the way from Minneapolis to Tokyo or Amsterdam is no small feat! Now these days, her two children enjoy that affirmation and love. Her husband of more than twenty years can tell you on any given day exactly how many *days* he has been married to this lovely lady.

But even she owes her great heart and self-confidence to someone from long ago.

DANCING FOR GRANDPA

IN THE BUSY HOUSE where I grew up—eight of us children were born within a twelve-year period—I was number five. I knew I was loved by both my parents, but there was always so much to get done. Large meals to make, stacks of dishes to wash, a garden to be weeded . . . the list went on and on.

As a result, leisurely bedtime stories or helping with a child's homework was a luxury that neither parent could afford. The ideal of "one-on-one" time was something for other families, not ours.

Except when I was with my grandfather. My dad's dad was our only remaining link to the family legacy, since the other three grandparents had already passed away. A happy man with a big smile, he naturally loved relating to people; that's what made him successful in the restaurant business. He also loved music—and so did I. He always seemed to be singing.

Whenever we'd be together at a family gathering, in the midst of the chaos he would ask me to dance while he sang some pop tune of the day. It made me feel so significant, at least to him. I didn't really know how to dance other than imitating what I saw in the skits on *The Carol Burnett Show.* But I loved the rhythm part of music. (I was forever pestering my parents for drum lessons, and they kept insisting I take "just one more year of piano" instead.)

With my grandpa, the spotlight was on me for one shining moment. We'd get to the end of a song, and he would throw his head back and laugh, his eyes dancing, his mouth wide open, and his hands clapping for joy. I would gaze at his lower teeth that seemed to rise to a peak in the middle, like a mountain ridge, and simply shiver with delight. In that moment, I would marvel that I—little third-grade Jennifer—could evoke so much pleasure in a grown-up. I felt so free, so valued, so celebrated.

I can't recall the songs he sang. I don't even remember the compliments he may have offered, such as "Good job!" I just recall basking in the warmth of his approval.

Grandpa died when I was in fifth grade. But the esteem he had shown for me, in a sea of brothers and sisters, was permanently rooted. How good it made me feel to know that there was something inside of me that somebody else had noticed.

The older I became, the more I wanted to do for other people what Grandpa had done for me—to find something about them to appreciate. Why? Because I had been treasured myself.

Oh, if only all grandpas and dads could be like that. Can you imagine?

Beneath the Surface

Sadly, they are not. And just as a minute of dancing for a loving grandpa can bring a lifetime of delightful memories at being so valued and cherished, mere minutes with a cruel or abusing one can go just as powerfully the other way. We do not always know the path that has brought a person to stand before us. We wonder why they always seem so angry. Why don't they ever have a kind word to speak? Why are they always so critical of others? We don't want to be around people like that, and we find ways to avoid them.

But there is always a reason, maybe even a "just a minute" reason, why they are the way they are.

The great American poet Henry Wadsworth Longfellow once wrote, "If we could read the secret history of our enemies, we should find in each man's life sorrow and suffering enough to disarm all hostility." That is why Jesus so courageously called us to go against the culture and "Love your enemies" (Matthew 5:44). He could see deep into the souls of those around Him, often the rejects of society. He knew what lay beneath the surface.

Toga Boy

Adolf Hitler was arguably the most hateful, destructive person in human history, and nothing can justify his unspeakably tragic actions. But even he, believe it or not, had his minute . . . a minute that helps to explain much. The son of a retired customs inspection officer with a drinking problem, he was one of five children in the house. His mother took him to church, where he sang in the choir and even considered becoming a priest at one point. But whenever his father beat him and his siblings, young Adolf's concerns were mainly just to survive until he could go out on his own.

His older half-brother seemed to get the worst of it for a while, until he finally ran away from home at age fourteen. This left a frustrated father to take out his irritation on the next

> **We can almost hear him deciding,** *They'll never make fun of me again!*

in line. Beatings were common. Arguments raged. His sister Paula wrote years later that Adolf "challenged my father to extreme harshness and . . . got his sound thrashing every day. He was a scrubby little rogue."

Seeing no options, the boy decided he would run away, too. His father caught wind of his plans and locked him upstairs. Then . . .

During the night Adolf tried to squeeze through the barred window. He couldn't quite make it, so took off his clothes. As he was wriggling his way to freedom, he heard his father's footsteps on the stairs and hastily withdrew, draping his nakedness with a tablecloth.

This time Alois [his father] did not punish with a whipping. Instead he burst into laughter and shouted to Klara [his mother] to come up and look at the "toga boy." The ridicule hurt Adolf more than any switch. . . .[8]

Is it any wonder that this boy resolved in his young spirit to be tougher and stronger than any foe? We can almost hear him deciding, *They'll never make fun of me again! No more embarrassment! I will be the master of my fate, my future, my nation, my race. Weakness and vulnerability shall never again be my lot.* And what a price the world ended up paying for one person's abuse.

Lucifer's Lies

A child's sense of self-worth is a foundation block upon which much of the rest of life rests. Delicately balanced, it is a thing of true beauty. But as we've seen, it can very quickly be thrown askew.

This is a favorite playground of Satan. If children think too little of themselves, their contribution to the world (barring a moment of intervention) is pretty much stunted. But too much self-esteem and pride can wreak havoc over time and space as well. Either way, the forces of evil win.

This issue of self-worth was the Achilles' heel that doomed Lucifer so long ago. This proud, resentful "angel of light" was thrown from the splendor of heaven. He and his massive ego made a huge feathery thud before the earth was even created. It is my observation that he has never forgotten his humiliation and what caused it. And this instrument has joined his tool bag ever since. It's not his only tool, but certainly his favorite.

As he watched the creation drama unfold, he was ever looking for the chink in God's armor to return and defeat Him. He saw plenty of God's heart during that wonderful process. He saw the Almighty's huge pleasure at light shining through the eternal darkness. He waited as solid, fertile ground rose up from the watery depths. Satan watched from the newly created shadows. Then on the sixth day, God scooped up some dirt and created the crown of everything: human beings. He didn't just speak Adam into existence like the rest of creation: He lovingly fashioned him in His very own image. He then breathed His very own breath into the man's nostrils, so that man became a living being. And God fell in love. . . .

Satan's conclusion? In my imagination, I can hear him saying to himself, "Okay, I've got the target. Now when and how to attack?" His answer: "The sooner the better—when the spirits of little people are still under construction. I'll attack when they're still moist, pliable, impressionable—before the cement fully sets.

"And through what method? I know! The same way I was destroyed. I will attack the child's very sense of worth. They must never grasp how much they are loved, how uniquely designed is their place in this world, the divine plans already awaiting them. Their little newly formed sense of worth—shall I push it too high like mine? Or drive it too low with hurt and abuse? Actually, both will work."

Of course I cannot document this silent soliloquy. All I can do is look at the evidence of Satan's work over the centuries. He has been relentless in warping the self-image of children, telling them lies about who they are and what they are worth.

It is up to us to set the record straight.

Section Three

A MOMENT TO FORM CHARACTER

As we move rapidly through the brief span of life we call "childhood," the cement of our spirits begins to harden. What has been imprinted there in our earliest memories becomes more and more permanent, simply a part of who we are.

By the adolescent years, it gets increasingly harder to make an impression. Where once only a small amount of fingerprint pressure was required, it now takes more like a hammer and chisel to reshape us. Wait until we are all grown up and . . . well, only a blast of dynamite will change our opinion or, harder still, behavior.

And, heaven help you when you get along to my age, at which . . . you just know what you know! My long-suffering wife, Donna, has rolled her eyes knowingly at my equally long-suffering executive assistant, Angie, and said, "He's often wrong, but never in doubt!"

Seriously, we must never underestimate the importance of investing in the young. Noted missionary and college president George S. Benson phrased it well: "Ideals and principles continue from generation to generation only when they are built into the hearts of children as they grow up."[9]

But this will not happen effortlessly. And children will not take the initiative. Think of it: They certainly have no voice to call for training, no organization or lobbying know-how, no political savvy, no financial resources, no vote to advance their needs. They have no money beyond a few sticky pennies, which explains how they get left off our national and church priorities, budgets, and agenda. They can't even read the newspaper or grasp the madness on the evening news. Yet there they are, nearly half our world's population—voiceless.

Children simply watch as we pile up national debt for them to pay and greedily foul our environment for them to someday clean up. Helplessly they watch as we destroy long-held values and character that once were our great strengths, the very fabric of nations. The smallest, weakest citizens among us are truly the ultimate victims of our selfishness and excesses of every kind. Worldwide, they are clearly the poorest of the poor.

But there is still hope. If we will seize our responsibility to lovingly shape their values and character, we can still affect the future. In the stories of this section you will see how powerfully word and deed can be brought together, in just a moment. And when they are . . . it's magic!

Self-esteem, about which we wrote in the last section, can be a frightening thing to behold without the guidance of values and character building. But watch what happens when we forge these vital qualities:

Integrity

THE GREATEST FISH

HE WAS ELEVEN years old, and went fishing every chance he got from the dock at his family's cabin on an island in the middle of a New Hampshire lake.

On the day before the bass season opened, he and his father were fishing early in the evening, catching sunfish and perch with worms. Then he tied on a small silver lure and practiced casting. The lure struck the water and caused colored ripples in the sunset, then silver ripples as the moon rose over the lake.

When his pole doubled over, he knew something huge was on the other end. His father watched with admiration as the boy skillfully worked the fish alongside the dock.

Finally he very gingerly lifted the exhausted fish from the water. It was the largest one he had ever seen, but it was a bass.

The boy and his father looked at the handsome fish, gills playing back and forth in the moonlight. The father lit a match and looked at his watch. It was 10 p.m.—two hours before the season opened. He looked at the fish, then at the boy.

"You'll have to put it back, son," he said.

"Dad!" cried the boy.

"There will be other fish," said his father.

"Not as big as this one," said the boy.

He looked around the lake. No other fishermen or boats were anywhere around in the moonlight. He looked again at his father.

Even though no one had seen them, nor could anyone ever know what time he caught the fish, the boy could tell by the clarity of his father's voice that the decision was not negotiable. He slowly worked the hook out of the lip of the huge bass and lowered it back into the black water.

The creature swished its powerful body and disappeared. The boy suspected that he would never again see such a great fish.

That was thirty-four years ago. Today, the boy is a successful architect in New York City. His father's cabin is still there on the island in the middle of the lake. He takes his own son and daughter fishing from the same dock.

And he was right. He has never again caught such a magnificent fish as the one he landed that night long ago. But he does see that same fish—again and again—every time he comes up against a question of ethics.

For, as his father taught him, ethics are simple matters of right and wrong. It is only the practice of ethics that is difficult. Do we do right when no one is looking? Do we refuse to cut corners to get the design in on time? Or refuse to trade stocks based on information that we know we aren't supposed to have?

We would if we were taught to put the fish back when we were young. For we would have learned the truth.[10]

If you lack integrity, you lack everything. If you cannot be trusted, you have nothing to offer.

I had the privilege of hearing one of the most respected leaders of our time at a conference, four-star General Colin Powell. His credits are awe-inspiring: wounded veteran of the Vietnam War, winner of the Bronze Star and the Purple Heart, former National Security Advisor, then Chairman of the Joint Chiefs of Staff, finally Secretary of State. When asked on this occasion about his role models, he didn't name any particular military heroes; instead he said, "My parents, aunts and uncles" along with his minister and teachers. "If these people hadn't been in my life when I was a child, I don't know where I would have ended up. They kept me in place. They passed on a hundred previous generations of experience."

I got a fuller picture once I read a particular moment in his powerful biography, *My American Journey*. He was in his mid-teen years. His parents, both immigrants from Jamaica, were raising him and his sister in the South Bronx.

OWNING UP TO THE TRUTH

SUNDAYS MEANT ATTENDING St. Margaret's [Episcopal] church, where we had our own family pew. Pop was senior warden, Mom headed the altar guild, and Marilyn [sister] played the piano at children's services. I was an acolyte. . . .

One summer in the early fifties, Father Weeden selected me, the son of two pillars of St. Margaret's, to go to a church camp near Peekskill. Once there, I promptly fell into bad company. One night, my newfound friends and I snuck out to buy beer. We hid it in the toilet tank to cool, but our cache was quickly discovered.

The priest in charge summoned all campers to the meeting hall.

He did not threaten or berate us. Instead, he asked who was ready to accept responsibility. Who would own up like a man?

We could probably have gotten away with our transgression by saying nothing. But his words struck me. I stood up. "Father, I did it," I said. When they heard me, two more budding hoodlums rose up and also confessed.

We were put on the next train back to New York. Word of our sinning preceded us. I dragged myself up Westchester Avenue and turned right onto Kelly Street like a felon mounting the gallows. As I reached number 952, there was Mom, whose usually placid face twisted into a menacing scowl. When she finished laying into me, Pop began.

Just when I thought I was eternally damned, Father Weeden telephoned. Yes, the boys had behaved badly, he said. "But your Colin stood up and took responsibility. And his example spurred the other boys to admit their guilt."

My parents beamed. From juvenile delinquent, I had been catapulted to hero. Something from that boyhood experience, the rewards of honesty, hit home and stayed.[11]

So *that's* why we as a nation came to have confidence in Colin Powell as a straight shooter we could trust. He learned early that truthfulness was the best policy. And the adults surrounding him rewarded that approach. They reinforced that he should speak the facts and let the chips fall where they may. It became a lifelong pattern for a great man.

Compassion

Of course we want our children to embrace the character trait of compassion. But being compassionate isn't always what it seems. Jesus told His followers, "You must be compassionate, just as your Father is compassionate" (Luke 6:36 NLT). What did He mean?

Compassion is a powerful word. As president of an organization that uses that name, I've naturally thought about it a bit over the years. I've told our staff that our greatest challenge is to live up to our name.

At first glance the word sounds very warmhearted and simple. Who of us doesn't intend to be compassionate? Surely this is just part of being a good human being, right? Nobody has anything against compassion.

> **Compassion flies in the face of all that is normally human.**

But if it's that natural, why did Jesus—who was always teaching radical, countercultural concepts—feel compelled to do more than just tell stories and parables about being compassionate? Why did He form a direct command, "You must be compassionate"?

I think it was because compassion actually flies in the face of all that is normally human. The Latin roots are *cum* and *pati*. The first word is easy to translate; it means "with" (as in *community* or *communication*). But "with" what? The *pati* part is the tough one. It means "to suffer." That's why the agony of Jesus leading up to the crucifixion is called "Passion Week."

Jesus' commandment essentially said, "I'm asking you to do something you really don't want to do—something your society rejects and has sought to escape at any cost." It's not enough just to do good, to solve other people's problems. He's asking more. He wants us to do a U-turn and go back against the tide, to walk courageously into the suffering. To weep with those who weep. To be weak with those who are weak. To be vulnerable alongside the vulnerable. Whoa, that is more than most people who just want to "do good" bargained for.

Think that's bad? When we move from Latin even further back to Greek (the language of the New Testament), one of the words is *splagchnizomai,* as in "When He saw the multitudes, He was *moved with compassion* for them, because they were weary and scattered, like sheep having no shepherd" (Matthew 9:36 NKJV, italics added). It signifies "to get worked up, to feel something deep in the gut," even to be outraged, angry, daring. This is the word the Greek playwrights used to depict warhorses—huge, powerful fighting beasts trained and covered in armor, trembling on the brink of battle, eager to charge into the fray, to attack. It is the same word used in the story of the Master confronting the horrible disease of leprosy: "Jesus was *indignant*. He reached out his hand and touched the man. 'I am willing,' he said. 'Be clean!'" (Mark 1:41, italics added).

Put those two concepts together, and you have what was going on deep in the heart of one particular compassionate father, as told by William Frey, former Episcopal bishop of Colorado (1973–89).

THE STORM WINDOWS

WHEN I WAS an undergraduate, I spent a couple of hours a week reading to a fellow student. His name was John, and he was blind.

One day I asked him how he had lost his sight. He told me of an accident that happened when he was a teenager and how at that point that he had simply given up on life. "When I knew I would never see again, I felt that life had ended as far as I was concerned. I was bitter and angry with God for letting it happen, and I took my anger out on everyone around me. I felt that since I had no future I wouldn't lift a finger on my own behalf. Let others wait on me. I shut my bedroom door and refused to come out except for meals."

I knew this man was now an eager learner and an earnest student, so I had to ask what had changed his attitude. He told me this story. "One day, in exasperation my father came into my room and started giving me a lecture. He said he was tired of my feeling sorry for myself. He said that winter was coming—and it was my job to put up the storm windows. 'You get those windows up by suppertime tonight or else!' he shouted, slamming the door on his way out."

"Well," said John, "that made me so angry that I resolved to do it! Muttering and cursing to myself, I groped my way out to the garage, found the windows, a stepladder, all the necessary tools, and went to work. *They'll be sorry when I fall off this ladder and break my neck*, I thought. *Then they'll have a kid who's blind and paralyzed!*

"But little by little, feeling my way around the house, I got the job done."

Then John paused . . . and his sightless eyes misted up as he told me, "I later discovered that at no time during the day had my father ever been more than four or five feet from my side."

Was this father compassionate? I say yes. He stayed home from work that day to do for his stricken son what was truly needed. He was preparing him to cope with real life, rather than remaining hopelessly dependent.

Sure, it was hard. The father may have debated with himself more than once about the wisdom of his act. But in the end, he could take assurance that he had built confidence into his son. He was forming his character for the years ahead.

Patience

A third trait our children don't naturally have, but desperately need, is patience—calm in the storm. We all wish they wouldn't erupt so quickly when life frustrates them. We want them to be able to hold their tongues. How do we instill this value?

One of my heroes is Tony Dungy, former coach of the world champion Indianapolis Colts, the first African-American coach to win a Super Bowl (2007). Now, you have to understand, I live in a house full of women—a wife and two daughters—whom I have miserably failed to excite regarding the world of sports. I really don't care whether they love balls, bats, hoops, and pigskin . . . but deep within athletics reside some of life's greatest examples of character. And nobody stands like such a rock, an eye of calm and patience in the middle of the storm, more than Tony Dungy. He's the master of composure.

He personifies those famous lines in Rudyard Kipling's poem:

> *If you can keep your head when all about you*
> *are losing theirs and blaming it on you. . . .*
> *If you can meet with triumph and disaster*

and treat those two imposters just the same. . . .
Yours is the Earth and everything that's in it,
and—which is more—you'll be a Man my son!

Where did Tony Dungy's spirit of calm come from? In his book *Quiet Strength,* he explains. And sure enough, it all came down to a minute—a rather painful minute.

THE CASTING LESSON

MY DAD WAS USUALLY a quiet, thoughtful man. A scientist at heart and by training, Wilbur Dungy loved to be outside, enjoying the scenery. Fishing allowed him time to contemplate, to listen, and to marvel at God's creation. My dad used fishing to teach his children to appreciate the everyday wonders of the world God created—the sandy shoreline, the dark, pine forests, the shimmering water, and the abundant wildlife. The lessons were always memorable, whether we caught a lot of fish or not.

Although we fished countless times together throughout our lives, one particular day stands out in my mind. It was a summer day in 1965. Summers in Michigan are beautiful, with comfortable temperatures and clear, blue skies. I was nine years old, and my brother was five. My dad had taken us fishing at one of the many small lakes around Jackson. On that day, my dad was teaching my brother and me how to cast. We were both working on it, mostly in silence, until my dad's voice finally broke a period of stillness.

"Hey, Linden, don't move for a minute, please." I looked back and watched my dad move his hand toward his face. Calm and deliberate, he continued to speak.

"Now, Linden, always make sure that you know not only where your pole is when you're starting to cast"—at this point, I realized my dad was working my brother's hook out of his own ear—"but also make certain that you know where everyone else is around you."

I learned something about proper casting that day, but I also learned something about patience. Years later, when I got hooked myself, in my hand, I realized *how much it hurts.* Remembering my dad's patience that day when Linden's hook was caught in his ear, I finally understood the importance of staying calm and communicating clearly.[12]

No wonder Tony Dungy could keep his cool in the heat of an NFL game! That's the kind of self-control we want for all our children. But it has to be modeled.

Purity

No area of values and character is more severely under attack in our society than the challenge for a young person to remain pure until their wedding day. To even pen those words seems ridiculously old-fashioned. Many, even in the church, who get their marching orders straight from the Bible, seem to have given up the impossible quest, waved the white flag, and surrendered their children to the inevitable. They have retreated to "damage control."

But before you cast any stones, consider the odds stacked against the children of today.

- Ten million adults (8 percent of U.S. coupled households) are cohabiting with a partner of the opposite sex.
- MTV is watched by 73 percent of boys and 78 percent of girls ages twelve to nineteen. The network averages thirteen sexual scenes per hour.
- There are 4.2 million pornography websites containing 372 million pages of porn, tapped by 68 million Internet searches each day. The average age of first exposure to Internet porn is eleven.

One of my dearest friends is Rebecca St. James, the popular Christian singer who has stood courageously, often totally alone, in her faithful quest to challenge youth to purity. This beautiful woman, yes inside and out, sings a powerful song, "Wait for Me" that has given strength and hope to a generation of girls. It was my privilege not long ago to attend her wedding—at age thirty-three.

Another good friend of mine tells how his attitude about sexual purity was fortified in his teen years by a "just a minute" challenge from a man he admired.

SHORT TALK ON THE STEPS

THE LITTLE COUNTRY CHURCH where I grew up, on a gravel road in northwest Pennsylvania, wasn't big enough to have a full-blown youth group. We met occasionally, and of course we had a Sunday school class; otherwise we sat with our parents in the worship services and just about anything else that took place.

But we did get to go to youth camp in the summer, which is where I first met Pastor Rex Moleen. A big man in his fifties who also worked for the state highway department, he was our cabin counselor—the grown-up charged with keeping us in line and, hopefully, teaching us something about God.

Then our pastor moved away, and in time I found out that Mr. Moleen would be driving the twenty miles or so from his home to fill in at our church temporarily. I was happy about that. The other teenagers and I could relate to him.

One Sunday morning after the service, he and I happened to be going down the four or five steps from the front door to the parking area. He greeted me with a smile. "Hi, Bill! How're you doing today?"

"Fine, Pastor Rex," I answered.

"How's school going?"

"Okay," I replied. "There sure is lots to do, though, along with the work at home." (My family ran a dairy farm just across the state line into New York, which kept my two older brothers and me plenty busy.)

"Any time for a girlfriend?" he asked with a twinkle in his eye.

"Oh, well . . . sure!" I replied with a grin. "There's always time for that, right?" I didn't feel like volunteering any further details, however, with other church people on the steps—including my mom.

"Well, let me just say," Pastor Rex answered, looking straight into my eyes, "that it's really an important thing to remain sexually pure until marriage. That would be a great gift to the girl who becomes your wife someday. It's an important value for you to hold as a young man living for Christ." He wasn't suspicious, or responding to any rumor he had heard about me; he was just being a shepherd of my young soul and conduct.

I nodded my agreement. I wasn't put off by his forthrightness; I took it at face value, as worthwhile advice from a man I respected. In fact, it cemented the conviction I already held on the inside. It made me say, *Yes, I'm really committed to that.*

The whole conversation was over in less than three minutes. Nothing more was said. But throughout the rest of high school and on into my college days at LeTourneau University in east Texas, I would think back to the resolve I had affirmed that Sunday noon in the Pennsylvania hills. In my mind I would replay that exchange. I'd given that man my word, and I wouldn't dare compromise it.

In my senior year I met a freshman named Nan, who has now been my wife for more than forty years. The gift of purity that we presented to each other on our wedding day was a precious thing that we still value. I've done a lot of work since then with business and ministry leaders, some of whom have derailed their usefulness to God and their companies through sexual misadventures, forfeiting their families. I've wished for them that, long ago, they too could have met Pastor Rex.

—BILL ANDERSON

Bill Anderson is a recognized leader in Christian publishing, having served thirty-one years with CBA (Christian Booksellers Association), twenty-four of those as president and CEO. He is now an independent life coach and executive mentor.

He is an example of stability forged early by an adult who was willing to speak up on a delicate subject. Someone cared enough to invest in young Bill Anderson's life and values. And it took only a moment.

True Beauty

While we're on the subject . . . let's talk about helping kids understand what true beauty is. After all, misconceptions abound. It's been a problem as old as time.

Beauty can be used for great good or great evil. The Bible records the story of beautiful Esther, the winner of an amazingly elaborate beauty contest to become the Persian queen. But, when her people, the Jews, were in grave danger of annihilation, this young woman—well coached by the godly Mordecai—used her beauty to beseech the king to spare them. It was risky, to be sure. She didn't hesitate.

Not all queens, however, were so noble and selfless. The wife of King Herod, in the time of Jesus, was a "beauty" named Herodias. She had an apparently gorgeous daughter named Salome. Herodias groomed her daughter's appearance and talent. She taught Salome to use her beauty and ability to dance for men to gain basically whatever she wanted. In the gospels of both Matthew and Mark we read the tragic story of how this princess put on such a show at a banquet thrown by the king that he foolishly (maybe a bit tipsily) promised the girl anything she wanted. "Whatever you ask I will give you, up to half my kingdom" (Mark 6:23).

The girl replied, in essence, "Just a minute." She consulted with her mother behind the curtain. The outcome was an absolute atrocity, as the head of her archenemy, John the Baptist, was soon served up on a platter!

What lessons do you think young, impressionable Salome took away from this minute in her life? What conclusions about men . . . women . . . justice . . . power . . . sexuality? As E. Stanley Jones says in his classic devotional, *Victorious Living,* regarding this passage, "The story of the young dancer in Herod's court is the story of 'the prodigal daughter,' the counterpart to 'the prodigal son.' . . . The prodigal son eventually came back, because he had a good father. The prodigal daughter never came back, because she had a bad mother."[13]

Basically Esther and Herodias were "the beauty and the beast," way ahead of their time. But it shows how horribly awry beauty can go still today. I am convinced that no generation in history has had to struggle with such a twisted, distorted view of "beauty" thrust upon it. We are bombarded all day long in magazines, movies, and TV commercials with skinny, shallow "Barbie"-style models that send our little girls' heads spinning. They look in the mirror and worry, obsessing over clothing, makeup, and hairdos, in a never-ending quest for a false, unrealistic, unattainable myth. My heart aches every time I hear of a young girl who has starved herself to an early death. She has given up not just food, but joy, peace, and the right to a happy childhood.

As a father of two beautiful daughters, I constantly sought to delight in their appearance, little angels growing more stunning with each passing year, and at the same time tried to steer their equally beautiful hearts in the right direction. My wife and I were clearly paddling the canoe upstream in our society. But the Scriptures could not have been clearer on this: "People look at the outward appearance, but the Lord looks at the heart" (1 Samuel 16:7).

Witness the courageous struggle of two loving mothers to instill within their daughters a true sense of beauty:

BEAUTIFUL ON THE INSIDE

LISA, MY TWO-YEAR-old daughter, and I were walking down the street toward home one sunny morning when two elderly women stopped in front of us. Smiling down at Lisa, one of them said, "Do you know you are a very beautiful little girl?"

Sighing and putting her hand on her hip, Lisa replied in a bored voice, "Yes, I know!"

A bit embarrassed, I apologized to the two ladies, and we continued our walk home, me thinking about how I would handle this situation. Once we got home I said to Lisa, "Lisa, when those two ladies spoke to you, they were talking about how pretty you are on the outside. It's true you are pretty on the outside. That's how God made you. But a person needs to be beautiful on the inside, too." As she looked at me uncomprehendingly, I continued.

"Do you want to know how a person is beautiful on the inside?" She nodded solemnly.

"Okay. Being beautiful on the inside is a choice you make, honey, to be good to your parents, a good sister to your brother, and a good friend to the children you play with. You have to care about other people, honey. You have to share your toys with your playmates. You need to be caring and loving when someone is in trouble or gets hurt and needs a friend. When you do all those things, you are beautiful on the inside. Do you understand what I'm saying?"

"Yes, Mommy. I'm sorry I didn't know that," she replied.

Hugging her, I told her I loved her and that I didn't want her to forget what I'd said. The subject never came up again.

Nearly two years later, we moved from the city to the country and enrolled Lisa in a preschool program. In her class was a girl named Jeanna, whose mother had died. The child's father had recently remarried, and it was readily apparent that Jeanna and her stepmom had a wonderful, loving relationship.

One day Lisa asked if Jeanna could come over to play for an afternoon, so I made arrangements with her stepmother to take Jeanna home with us the next day after the morning session.

As we were leaving the parking lot the following day, Jeanna said, "Can we go see my mommy?"

I knew her stepmother was working, so I said cheerfully, "Sure, do you know how to get there?" Jeanna said she did. Following her directions, I soon found myself driving up the gravel road into the cemetery.

My first response was one of alarm, as I thought of the possible negative reaction of Jeanna's parents when they learned what had happened. However, it was obvious that visiting her mother's grave was very important to her, something she needed to do; and she was trusting me to take her there. Refusing would send her a message that it was wrong of her to want to go there.

Outwardly calm, as though I'd known this was where we were going all along, I asked, "Jeanna, do you know where your mother's grave is?"

"I know about where it is," she responded.

I parked on the road in an area she indicated, and we looked around until I found a grave with her mother's name on a small marker.

We sat down next to it. Jeanna started talking about events before her mother's death, as well as what had happened on the day she died. She spoke for some time. All the while Lisa, weeping, had her arms around Jeanna and, patting her gently, said over and over, "Oh, Jeanna, I'm so sorry. I'm so sorry your mother died."

Finally, Jeanna looked at me and said, "You know, I still love my mommy, and I love my new mommy, too."

Deep in my heart, I knew that this was the reason she'd asked to come here. Smiling down at her, I said, "You know, Jeanna, that's the wonderful thing about love. You never have to take it away from one person to give it to another. There's always more than enough to go around. It's kind of like a giant rubber band that stretches to surround all the people you care about." I continued, "It's perfectly fine and right for you to love both your mothers. I'm sure your own mother is very glad that you have a new mommy to love you and take care of you and your sisters."

Smiling back at me, she appeared satisfied with my response. We sat quietly for a few moments, and then we all stood up, brushed ourselves off, and went home. The girls played happily after lunch until Jeanna's stepmother came to pick her up.

Briefly, without going into a lot of detail, I told her what had occurred that afternoon and why I'd handled things as I had. To my profound relief, she was very understanding and appreciative.

After they left, I picked Lisa up in my arms, sat down on a kitchen chair, kissed her cheek, and hugged her, saying, "Lisa, I'm so proud of you. You were such a wonderful friend to Jeanna this afternoon. I know it meant a lot to her that you were so understanding and that you cared so much and felt her sadness."

A pair of lovely, dark brown eyes looked seriously into mine as my daughter asked, "Mommy, was I beautiful on the inside?"[14]

—PAMELA J. DEROY

MAKE A WISH

I'LL NEVER FORGET the day Momma *made* me go to a birthday party. I was in Mrs. Black's third-grade class in Wichita Falls, Texas, and I brought home a slightly peanut-buttery invitation.

"I'm not going," I said. "She's a new girl named Ruth, and Berniece and Pat aren't going. She asked the whole class, all thirty-six of us."

As Momma studied the handmade invitation, she looked strangely sad. Then she announced, "Well, you are going! I'll pick up a present tomorrow."

I couldn't believe it. Momma had never made me go to a party! I was positive I'd just die if I had to go. But no amount of hysterics could sway Momma.

When Saturday arrived, Momma rushed me out of bed and made me wrap the pretty pink pearlized mirror-brush-and-comb set she'd bought. She drove me over in her yellow and white 1950 Oldsmobile. Ruth answered the door and motioned me to follow her up the steepest, scariest staircase I'd ever seen.

Stepping through the door brought great relief. The hardwood floors gleamed in the sun-filled parlor. Snow-white doilies covered the backs and arms of well-worn overstuffed furniture.

The biggest cake I ever saw sat on one table. It was decorated with nine pink candles, a messily printed "Happy Birthday Ruthey," and what I think were supposed to be rosebuds.

Thirty-six Dixie cups filled with homemade fudge were near the cake—each one with a name on it.

This won't be too awful—once everyone gets here, I decided.

"Where's your mom?" I asked Ruth.

Looking down at the floor, she said, "Well, she's sorta sick."

"Oh. Where's your dad?"

"He's gone."

Then there was a silence, except for a few raspy coughs from behind a closed door. Some fifteen minutes passed . . . then ten more. Suddenly the terrifying realization set in. *No one else was coming.* How could I get out of here? As I sank into self-pity, I heard muffled sobs. Looking up, I saw Ruth's tear-streaked face. All at once my eight-year-old heart was overwhelmed with sympathy for Ruth and filled with rage at my thirty-five selfish classmates.

Springing to my white-patent leather feet, I proclaimed at the top of my lungs, "Who needs 'em?"

Ruth's startled look changed to excited agreement.

There we were—two small girls and a triple-decker cake, thirty-six candy-filled Dixie cups, ice cream, gallons of red Kool-Aid, three dozen party favors, games to play and prizes to win.

We started with the cake. We couldn't find any matches, and Ruthey (she was no longer just plain Ruth) wouldn't disturb her mom, so we just pretended to light the candles. I sang "Happy Birthday" while Ruthey made a wish and blew out the imaginary flames.

In a flash it was noon. Momma was honking out front. Gathering up all my goodies and thanking Ruthey repeatedly, I dashed to the car. I was bubbling over.

"I won *all* the games! Well, really, Ruthey won Pin the Tail on the Donkey, but said it wasn't fair for the birthday girl to win a prize, so she gave it to me, and we split the party favors 50/50. Momma, she just loved the mirror set. I was the only one there—out of Mrs. Black's whole third-grade class. And I can't wait to tell every one of them what a great party they missed!"

Momma pulled over to the curb, stopped the car, and hugged me tight. With tears in her eyes, she said, "I'm so proud of you!"

That was the day I learned that one person could really make a difference. I had made a big difference in Ruthey's ninth birthday, and Momma had made a big difference in my life.[15]

—LeAnne Reeves

An Attitude of Gratitude

Here is another precious character value we can instill as a gift to the next generation. It is becoming a lost art. We sometimes weakly try to shore up the habit when our children receive something by chiming, "Billy, now what do you say?" But real gratefulness is something much deeper; it wells up from deep within. It's a worldview, a perception of one's self, an attitude, a spirit.

Perhaps it gets lost in the avalanche of "stuff" that bombards our children's lives in this wildly affluent society. But expressions of gratitude have become rare enough to be treasured and savored. They stand out nowadays, warming our hearts when we see or hear them.

My younger daughter, Katie, was the "gratitude queen" in our family. I honestly don't know where it came from in such extraordinary measure, but she consistently stopped Donna and me in our tracks. Her little voice would speak up from her car seat in the back, "Thank you for the hamburger, Mommy"—and a few seconds later, "Thank you for the French fries, Daddy." Huh?

Christmas presents were abandoned still half-wrapped as soon as she saw what it was, so Katie could come bounding across the living room in her pajamas to throw herself into our arms, bubbling with uncontainable thankfulness.

Sometimes we would confine prayers at bedtime just to thank-yous— "no fair asking God for anything tonight." Now, I may have been born at night, but I wasn't born last night. I'm on to the ol' stall-the-bedtime routine as long as possible. You know, the ploy of one more story, one more glass of water, one more question, one more hug. But Katie could sweetly and sincerely unearth so many things to thank God for that I could never find it in my heart to say, "Okay, Katie—that's enough. Amen!"

> **As I was about to take a sip, my peasant host asked softly and kindly, "Aren't we going to thank God for the coffee?"**

Perhaps the hardest part of my job as Compassion's president is traveling back and forth between the poor and rich parts of our world, often in the same day. I sometimes tell audiences, "I am called on one hand to *'comfort the afflicted'* and then just hours later to *'afflict the comfortable.'*" It breaks my heart these two parts of humanity don't know each other.

They are both wonderful, and, they really, urgently need what the other half has. Like gratitude. I remember being served a cup of coffee in an Ethiopian hut one time. As I was about to take a sip, my peasant host asked softly and kindly, "Aren't we going to thank God for the coffee?"

It was that kind of minute that launched the life of one of the world's greatest preachers when he was just a boy. Harry's father had died of typhoid fever in 1878 when Harry was just two years old, leaving a mother and her children in poverty. He remembered a time when she set the table in their humble Toronto home and poured water for them. No food, just water. She then asked young Harry to join her in giving thanks to God for at least the water.

That moment was the beginning of his spiritual heritage, one that included a passion for God's Word. It was a minute in time Harry never forgot. At age fourteen he completed reading the Bible not once, but fourteen times that year. Harry Ironside became a prominent preacher. His nearly

100 Bible commentaries were used for decades in colleges and seminaries across the continent by students—including me at Moody Bible Institute. Thousands of men and women listened spellbound as Harry related the Bible in simple, ordinary language.

Generosity

On the other side of the gratitude coin you'll always find generosity. If I have learned anything in my years at Compassion, I have learned that you cannot outgive God, and you cannot outgive the poor. Both will surprise and humble you with their delight in giving.

People who don't know the poor tend to think, "They don't have much of anything, so surely they must hoard what little they've got. They need it!" Actually, the opposite is true. The worst reputation you could get in the West African village where I grew up was to be selfish. To withhold from your brother or sister in time of need was, well, simply unthinkable. If you had it and they needed it . . . you gave it!

The opposite of poor is not rich . . . it's "enough." If no one has to have too much, everyone can have enough.

I love this story of the awakening moment for a young girl back in the Great Depression.

PROBLEM OR SOLUTION?

IT WAS 1933. I had been laid off my part-time job and could no longer make my contribution to the family pantry. Our only income was what Mother could make by doing dressmaking for others.

Then Mother got sick for a few weeks. The electric company came out and cut off the power when we couldn't pay the bill. The gas company cut off the gas. Then the water company—but the Health Department made them turn it back on for reasons of sanitation. The cupboard got very bare. Fortunately, we had a vegetable garden and were able to cook some of its produce in a campfire in the back yard.

Then one day my younger sister came tripping home from school with, "We're supposed to bring something to school tomorrow to give to the poor."

Mother started to blurt out, "I don't know of anyone who is any poorer than we are," when her mother, who was living with us at the time, shushed her with a hand on her arm and a frown.

"Eva," she said, "if you give that child the idea that she is 'poor folks' at her age, she will be 'poor folks' for the rest of her life. There is one jar of that homemade jelly left. She can take that."

Grandmother found some tissue paper and a little bit of pink ribbon with which she wrapped our last jar of jelly. Sis tripped off to school the next day proudly carrying her "gift to the poor."

And ever after, if there was a problem in the community, Sis just naturally assumed that she was supposed to be part of the solution.[16]

—EDGAR BLEDSOE

Kindness

Finally, another element of character is kindness. One of the most gentle-spirited people I know is Dean Merrill. As we wrote our last book together, I watched from across the table as this veteran writer's eyes would well up with tears as I told him the stories of my abuse at the hands of cruel, twisted boarding school houseparents. His jaw would clench and his hands would unconsciously form into fists as I relived my torment to capture it in the book. *He is a very compassionate man*, I thought as we met many times together. *I wonder where that comes from?*

Well, now I know. It came from a lifelong example of a gentle, warm-hearted father—as shown in this brief moment on a summer day at the county fair. Here it is, in Dean's own words.

RACE WITHOUT A FINISH

THE OGLE COUNTY FAIR was a wonderful place for a nine-year-old boy and his dad to spend a lazy summer afternoon. The midway with its towering Ferris wheel, the popcorn stands, the 4-H displays of everything from blackberry jam to Hereford steers . . . I loved it all. And my tall, black-haired father had taken the day off from his duties as pastor of a small-town Illinois church to show me a good time.

This was before the days of one-price entry fees; you had to pay a quarter or thirty-five cents for each ride. That meant I didn't get to go on more than three or four attractions, but I was still happy as we walked the dusty aisles and looked at the sights.

About three-thirty in the afternoon, the horse races began over at the big dirt oval. I knew my father was not about to get close to the gambling that went on there—but he loved horses. As a farm lad growing up, he had worked the fields with horse-drawn implements. He knew horseflesh better than anyone, I thought.

So we stood in the open grass outside the far end of the track, along the rail for the final turn. Several races went streaking by on their way to the finish line. The announcer's voice squawked over the PA system. I jumped up and down with excitement.

Then came the first of the harness races. One horse was in the lead, the second a length behind, and in third place another jockey was vigorously laying on the whip. "Go, go, go!" I yelled as the roar from the grandstand came to meet us across the track.

Suddenly, there was a jerk on my shirtsleeve.

"Come on—we're leaving!" my father snapped. His face was flushed. I couldn't figure out what was wrong. Normally a calm man, he was definitely upset.

"But, Dad—wait!"

"Come now."

"Can't we just see the end of the race? Please?"

"No."

We walked through the tall grass toward our old sedan. *What was the matter?* I couldn't make sense of anything.

Finally he said, "That fellow had been beating that horse since way back on the straightaway—and the horse was already giving him everything he had. *I won't stand by* and watch a man beat a horse like that! It's not right."

I looked up at his eye and almost thought I saw a tear. Little more was said as we drove the nine miles home. My father didn't try to make a point by adding, "Don't you ever do anything like that" or "Be sure to be kind to animals" or some other comment on the abuse of power. He didn't need to.

He had implanted a value in me so deeply I remember it to this day, decades later. He did it simply by being a man of principle himself.[17]

Section Four

A MOMENT TO DISCOVER TALENT

A plaque hangs in my office that reads "Nothing Done for a Child Is Ever Wasted." That is true, as we've seen, with regard to rescuing little ones from danger, to lifting their self-image, to influencing their character . . . and now, in this section, to recognizing the moment that can create a dream, inspire a talent, or unearth a deeply buried gifting. This ability, if found and nurtured, can launch a lifetime of joy, fulfillment, and even impact on the world that will go beyond your own lifetime or reach. Such a minute may well be your greatest contribution to the world.

I remember the minute my daughter Jenny's passion for theater was born. I was sitting in my armchair reading the paper after an exhausting day at the office. Donna was comfortably ensconced across the room reading a book. It was getting late. The mood was peaceful. Even five-year-old Jenny, up in her room, was strangely quiet—maybe too quiet. Her baby sister, Katie, was already down for the night.

All of a sudden this beautiful ballerina flew into the living room in an explosion of grand entrance, jumped nimbly up onto the coffee table, and struck a pose. "Ta-da!" she sang out. Donna and I looked up, startled, to see slender arms and legs, with a billowing pink tutu that refused to stay up and rustled with her every breath. It took over her little waist like a newly plucked dandelion. Her hair was topped with a sparkling tiara from last Halloween. Her eyes twinkled with excitement as she grinned from ear to ear. She stood poised, expectant . . . time stood still.

I was one breath away from mumbling, "Nice, Jenny—now take that off; it's time for bed." She had a track record, after all, for being the queen of late-night stall tactics. But for some reason, I reached up to twist the light on the pole lamp, turning it into her very first spotlight. Like a Ringling Brothers circus announcer, I boomed, "And now, ladies and gentlemen—the beautiful, the very talented, the famous . . . I give you Jenny Stafford!"

The little prima ballerina danced the performance of a lifetime. She was suddenly on the main stage of New York's Lincoln Center doing pirouettes, leaps, and spins. The crowd (Donna and I) sprang to our feet, cheering wildly with thunderous applause. The moment was magic; Jenny was hooked. A little girl's dream was born.

From that moment on, she jumped wholeheartedly into every drama production within her reach—voice and dance lessons, drama club and camps. In high school, she was Dolly in *Hello, Dolly!* In college she was Guinevere in *Camelot*. Along the way she developed a passion for other aspects of theater such as directing, producing, and writing. For two years after college, she toured to a new town each week with the Missoula Children's Theatre, acting and singing while also directing, teaching, and developing young actors. As she worked in Chicago theatre for a couple of years, her passion focused on the creative process of writing scripts and song lyrics for new musicals. She eventually chased this dream all the way to a master's degree in music theatre writing at New York University's Tisch School of the Arts. She is currently a theatre teaching artist with the Metropolitan Opera Guild in Manhattan.

That's all very exciting to a father's heart. I'm so glad I didn't make her take off that tutu and go straight to bed that night long ago.

The Sound of Music

It has been such fun over these last few years for me to reflect with people on this incredible power of a moment in children's lives. One time awhile back Andraé Crouch, the great seven-time Grammy Award winner known for such songs as "My Tribute (To God Be the Glory)," "Through It All," and "I Don't Know Why Jesus Loved Me," was visiting Compassion's headquarters in Colorado Springs. That night at supper when he heard my concept, he sat up excitedly. "Oh, oh, oh—I got one!"

Andraé had a terrible stutter when he was a boy in California. He could barely express himself when asked the simplest question. His twin sister Sandra, with a compassionate heart, used to jump in and mercifully answer for him, to the relief of the flustered boy. One time Andraé's father noticed that he didn't stutter when he was singing, especially Sunday school songs. His father said, "Andraé, when you are listening to people, imagine they are singing, and sing your answer back to them." It worked.

> "I looked up and down that row of keys . . . and I found myself. In a minute, I knew my place, my future."

That ability to hear music in the spoken word of others served him well as an adult in his prolific writing of songs. He told me, "I can remember vividly when a lady who was grieving the death of her beloved husband uttered the words, 'It won't be long till we'll be leavin' here.'" That became the lead line of his classic "It Won't Be Long," a precious song that has comforted many of us for decades.

But the crucial story—the "moment"—for Andraé Crouch came years earlier, when he was only eleven years old. His father pastored a small church in downtown Los Angeles. "It was just a handful of people, mainly homeless types. All I really remember is they all smelled like old cheese," he said.

There was no music in this little church. Andraé's father badly wanted some so they could really worship. But how? Then one day he had an idea. Kneeling down in front of his son, he said, "Andraé . . . if God gave you the gift of music, would you use it for His glory?" The boy could only reply, "Yes, Papa, I would."

The father went up and down their neighborhood until he found someone with an old upright piano in the basement. Taking his young son by the hand, he led him there. "I can still remember the musty smell, the creaking stairs, and the feel of my daddy's big hand."

Andraé took his seat on the rickety piano bench, still wondering what this was all about. His father reached over his shoulder and lifted up the lid, exposing the keys yellowed by neglect and time. Andraé told me, "I looked up and down that row of keys . . . and I found myself. In a minute, I knew my place, my future." Within mere weeks the young boy's gift had exploded, to the point that he was playing for church. His talent had been lying dormant, just waiting for that inspired minute to occur. And I for one am so grateful it happened.

Among the millions who have been blessed by Andraé Crouch's music is a woman who got off to a very hurtful start in her music. Remember the power of a moment to lift up? Well, the same amount of time can also tear down. In fact this memory is so painful that "Janet" has asked us not to use her real name.

"YOU CAN'T SING"

I WAS EXCITED from the minute I heard, in fourth grade, that our school was going to attempt an operetta—a children's version of the Gilbert and Sullivan classic *H.M.S. Pinafore.* Wouldn't it be fantastic if I could play the part of Josephine, the captain's daughter who falls in love with the common sailor Ralph Rackstraw?

I eagerly began preparing for auditions. One evening at home, I was bouncing around singing the tryout song, when my mother—an elementary schoolteacher herself—interrupted, *"Whatever* are you doing?"

"I'm getting ready for the musical at school!" I cheerfully replied. "I want to be Josephine!"

"Janet," she declared, lowering her gaze at me, "you can't sing— your brother got the voice in this family."

This icy retort was not unusual for my mother; she was a get-to-the-point kind of person who had endured tough times while growing up herself and tended now, as an adult, to call 'em as she saw them.

Life was meant to be hard, in her view.

Still, I gulped at her pronouncement. *Wow—I never knew that,*
I said to myself. If Mother said I had a lousy voice, then it must be
true. I laid aside the dream and told myself not to bother trying out.

As the years went by, I never again ventured toward the world of
music. I walled myself off from my mother, especially after the time I
was trying to pick out just the right outfit for a special occasion and
asked her to help me—and was told, "I don't have time to be concerned with your problems." Yes, she had a classroom to manage
plus three kids at home (I was the oldest). But would it have been so
burdensome to help match a dress and accessories?

I was more drawn toward my father's sunny, gregarious outlook
on life. I decided that whenever Mother saw the glass as half-empty,
I would call it half-full. I wanted to be the opposite of her, almost
needling her with my upbeat attitude.

It was long after I had finished high school, gone away to university, gotten married, and had two children of my own that something
nudged me toward forgotten territory. A guitar teacher was giving
my son his lesson in the other room of our house, and I absentmind-
edly hummed along with the popular song being played. At the end,
the teacher looked my way and said, "You really have a wide octave
range."

Who, me?

More years passed. I was working as an executive assistant for
a Christian publisher, and after a staff devotional period in which we
had sung a worship song together, a good friend about my age said,
"Janet, I love sitting next to you—you have such a rich, mellow alto
voice!"

"Really?"

"Yes, you do! And you can harmonize with the tune and everything. Lots of people can't do that."

I was shocked. Could it be that Mother was wrong back then,
thirty-five years before? How many thrilling moments had I missed

along the way? I would have loved to have sung in a church choir, for example. But I had always assumed I didn't have the gift for it.

Meanwhile, I've found other ways to excel. I've refused to play the victim role or carry a burden of resentment. I've tried to continue an optimistic attitude throughout the years in whatever I've done— even serving as my mother's primary caregiver during her last years until she passed away. God's design for me is something I seek to fulfill, to this day.

"Janet" is now in her sixties and works for a large trade association as events producer. She and her husband have four grandchildren, who receive abundant affirmation for their gifts.

I suppose it is because music so deeply touches the soul that, in looking for stories for this book, music kept popping up in life after life. Singer-songwriter-blogger Shaun Groves is my good friend. He wouldn't necessarily know that, since I tease him (and he me) mercilessly. He has a great sense of humor, a deep love for God, and a passion for life that leaves most of us in the dust. He has a huge heart of compassion for the poor; in fact, every week I learn of people who have sponsored children because of Shaun. Here is his "minute" story. . . .

TO BE A DORK?

I CAN REMEMBER hearing my father's baritone voice murmur through the Sheetrock and into my room after lights out. I crept from my bed and knelt in the hallway eavesdropping. My parents were sitting at the kitchen table shuffling through bills. I was too young to understand all that was being said but I caught enough to know there was a problem.

Now I know everyone has a month or year like that. It was probably no big deal. But back then it left me scared.

When I was a boy, on long road trips to visit relatives, I'd lie on the floor of the backseat singing to the thumpty-thump of the highway. In middle school I took up the saxophone. I'd practice an hour before school. At lunch I'd eat quickly and then practice until the class bell rang. After school, I spent another hour or so practicing. I loved music.

When high school rolled around I had to choose between that love and fear. My sister is five years older than me, gorgeous, charismatic, popular—though humble enough to tell you she's never been any of those things. Back then she was our family's resident expert on high school, and her word was gospel to me. According to her, guys in high school band were dorks and their lives were hard.

Now that I'm a parent, I understand well why my mom did what she did next. I'm constantly shielding my kids from the sharp pieces of life, reminding them to "be careful" and "watch out." My mom loved me like that too. For my safety, she agreed with my sister, but left the choice up to me.

Then she made a mistake. She let me work in my grandmother's flower shop that summer.

I told my grandmother how much I loved making music. I told her about what dorks the band guys were in high school. She asked me what my mom had to say, and I told her Mom thought being in band could make high school, already a hard thing, even harder for me.

"Your mom was in band," she said. "All your aunts and your Uncle Joel were in band."

I had no idea I was part of a band nerd legacy.

And my mom doesn't know this (until now), but somewhere in that conversation my grandmother told me not to listen to her daughter. She told me God gave me a gift, He made me a musician, and I had to be what He made me no matter what.

That's why I was in the high school band. Yes, I was a dork. But I had all the friends I needed, even if they weren't homecoming king material. It wasn't so bad.

I met my wife right after high school. I was nineteen and she was twenty-three, freshly graduated from college and on her way to grad school. We were just friends when she listed the requirements for her future husband—the man I desperately wanted to be. I was lacking one thing: a stable income. I knew music would likely never lead to stability. I thought about giving up music for Becky. I thought about just staying at the title company where I worked, being a business-man or maybe even a lawyer. I was stuck. So I stalled; went to junior college, and applied to music schools.

Two of my friends had older sisters who'd quit music school. They told me horror stories about how hard it was, and one even told me I could never do it. Life in a suit and tie was looking safer every day.

Then came the day our family gathered around my grandmother's bed and sang the hymns she'd rocked all of us to sleep with as kids. She was dying of cancer. One by one we told her good-bye. Her last words to me were "I'm proud of you. Don't be afraid."

I went to college and studied music composition. And it was hard—the hardest thing I've ever done. I got the girl too, who, by the time we were more than friends, had become a woman who loved me more than stability.

We married and moved to Nashville. My mom, understandably, worried that I didn't have a teacher's certificate to fall back on. But the choice was mine. I signed a record deal, dedicated my first album to my grandmother who spoke courage into me, and I've been making music for a living ever since.

There have been months when Becky and I have shuffled bills around on the kitchen table after lights out, deciding what we could pay and what would have to wait. But it's been worth it.

This story is for all of us who by now are thinking, "I too have missed an awful lot of opportunities to be that kind of hero for my own children" or the children who have passed through our lives. We all miss chances. It is my prayer that all of us become more alert to the children around us and be ready for such a moment.

But maybe, just maybe, you have created a moment you don't even know about. Like Lindsay Goodwin's father . . .

HAND ON THE SHOULDER

ONE OF THE FIRST TIMES I ever sang in church, I forgot my words, started crying, and hid inside the preacher's podium out of sheer embarrassment. I was really young, and I don't remember how it all ended. I think my dad came up and talked me out of the podium. I'm sure he carried me down to our pew and did his best to soothe my tears. Whatever he did, it didn't discourage me from singing in churches.

A few years later, I had been asked to sing at a church in another town for their revival services. This was the late Eighties or early Nineties, when we still used accompaniment tracks: cassette tapes that had the instrumental portion of the song recorded, sometimes in multiple keys, so a person could sing along . . . like Christian karaoke. If you had a multiple-key accompaniment track, you had to employ great caution to rewind, fast-forward, and STOP! the tape in *just* the right spot. *And* you had to make sure your cassette tape was inserted into the player on the right side. This way, your music would be queued and ready for you to sing.

On this night, however, not enough caution had been employed.

When the music started, it was in the track's highest key. When I began to sing, it sounded nothing like a human. I'm sure my eyes were full of panic. I still can't hold a proper poker face. As I continued to sing, pushing through my panic, my dad once again walked up to the stage, laid his hand on my shoulder, and started singing. The high key was perfect for a man's voice one octave lower, and his buttery baritone softened the harsh blow of my dying-cat soprano. Together, we sang these words. . . .

There's a hand, a hand on my shoulder
Through the storm, however it blows
There's a hand, a hand on my shoulder
Stays with me, wherever I go.
(from "Hand on My Shoulder" by Sandi Patti)

That moment, as much as any other in my childhood, sticks out to me. I was embarrassed, panicked, and afraid I wouldn't be able to finish. My dad, however, was calm and collected. He was there to encourage me and support me. He literally came up and stood beside me while I attempted the impossible.

A couple of months ago, my dad sat me down and said, "There's something I need to talk to you about. I'm afraid I didn't affirm you enough when you were younger."

So, I told him the truth:

"You probably didn't, Dad. But you did everything exactly right. I never doubted whether or not I was loved or supported growing up. You told me, as many times as you had the opportunity, that you loved me. And I knew it was true. Your actions backed it up."

So to every adult I say: Tell the children around you how much you value them. Encourage them every chance you get. When they attempt the impossible, take a chance and stand beside them. And whenever you can, tell them that you love them.

They'll never, ever forget it. I promise.

Before I move on, let me give you just one more music story. This one is about the pilgrimage of a dear friend of the Stafford family. I don't want to give away his age, but let's just say my parents, sister, and I stayed in the Ferrin house with Paul and Marjorie when I was just four years old, before we had even gone to Africa as missionaries in 1955. Paul is an accomplished musician and choral arranger, and has led music ministry in very large churches in such cities as Wichita, Memphis, Sacramento, and San Jose.

What this couple is doing now is precious to my heart. They lead community-wide hymn-sing events across the nation. Christians meet together, throw back their heads, and sing the great hymns that stirred our souls when we were children. "Number 363!" someone will shout out, just like in the good ol' days, and we sing "The Old Rugged Cross" in four-part harmony (remember that?). Such hymns still find their way into our minds in times of great sorrow, joy, or even the ordinary trials of life.

But when Paul was just learning to play, there was a crucial moment. . . .

SOMETHING'S MISSING

I BEGAN LESSONS as a four-year-old and was playing for services in my father's small-town church by the age of nine. When we moved to Denver five years later, I got to continue studying under one of the most outstanding teachers in the city, Mrs. Jones. She was an incredible artist with hymns and gospel songs, improvising the most dazzling embellishments as she went along—what we called "evangelistic style" in those days. I would see her at the keyboard for citywide crusades and simply be in awe of her talent.

But then came the day at my piano lesson when Mrs. Jones caught me off guard with an odd announcement. "I've taken you about as far as I can, Paul," she said in a serious tone. "You need more of a classical foundation. I want to turn you over to a colleague of mine who specializes in that field. She and I both teach at the same college."

I certainly didn't want to leave her instruction, but I agreed. For the next two years, I studied with the other teacher. I couldn't "improv" one extra note; I had to stick exactly to what was written on the page by Haydn, Chopin, or Liszt.

Then came a recital in downtown Denver where I would play "Traumerei" by the 19th-century German composer Robert Schumann, in the key of B (five sharps). It was difficult, to say the least. I managed to get through the piece without any major glitches.

At the end of the program, Mrs. Jones came up to me. She spoke the unvarnished truth. "You played that piece flawlessly," she said (which made me feel good for a second) "—but your heart wasn't in it. I'm ready to take you back."

"Okay!" I responded with a big grin. I would once again be able to focus on the kind of music I loved most. I studied with Mrs. Jones for the rest of high school and moved on after that to college study. As it has turned out, my entire ministry career has been invested in Christian music—with "heart."

Beyond the Keyboard—The Backboard

One of the most respected basketball coaches in the game is Pat Riley, currently president of the Miami Heat. Year after year, he has directed teams of thoroughbred, elite players—most notably the Lakers—to NBA championships. Who can forget him sitting on the front row of the Los Angeles Forum with his slicked-back hair, talent and tension strung out on either side, and surrounded by the glitz and glitter of Hollywood's most celebrated, highly opinionated, privileged class breathing down his neck? He seemed fearless, collected, confident no matter how tight the score or how high the stakes being played out in front of him.

How did Pat Riley get to be like that? Was he born that way? No, not even close. His transitional moment came when, as a nine-year-old whimpering, defeated little boy who hated basketball, he was gently lifted, in tears, from his hiding place in the family garage by a very wise and compassionate father. Read it in his own words from his book *The Winner Within*.

WHEN YOUR BACK IS AGAINST THE WALL

THE LOS ANGELES LAKERS were dominating the Boston Celtics in the final round of the 1984 National Basketball Association championship. We thrashed the Celtics in game one, on their home floor. We beat them by thirty-three points in game three. We were ahead by ten points in game four and cruising. Then it all changed.

Two days after losing the deciding seventh game, we were back in Los Angeles for our last team meeting. I looked at the young faces and said, "Even though we lost, they can't take away our pride or our dignity; we own those. We are not chokers or losers. We are champions who simply lost a championship."

We came back for the 1984–85 season sharply focused. All year long, we heard how we were the "showtime" team that folded as soon as things got rough. The Celtics and their fans referred to us as the L.A. Fakers. Abuse and sarcasm were heaped on, and we had to take it.

But we achieved a tremendous season, and ripped through the playoffs. On May 27, we got back to face our tormentor, the Celtics, in Boston Garden.

The next day's headlines called game one of the 1985 finals "The Memorial Day Massacre." A 148–114 humiliation was the most embarrassing game in the history of the Laker franchise. We saw ourselves becoming exactly what we had been called: choke artists, underachievers. *Why is it,* I wondered, *that every time we play the Celtics, we become paralyzed with fear?*

Before we went out on the floor for game two, we gathered in the dingy locker room of the Boston Garden. The players were sitting there, ready to listen and to believe.

Every now and then, you have your back pushed up against a wall. It seems there's nobody you can depend on but yourself. That's how the Lakers felt. If we lost, the choke reputation would be chiseled in stone, a permanent verdict. If we won, we had the opportunity to prove that we could keep on winning. It was a do-or-die situation.

I faced Kareem Abdul-Jabbar, our star center, and said, "When I saw you and your father on the bus today, it made me realize what this whole moment is about. You spent a lot of time with Big Al today. Maybe you needed that voice. Maybe everyone in this room needs to hear that kind of a voice right now—the voice of your dad, the voice of a teacher, the voice of somebody in the past who was there when you didn't think you could get the job done.

"A lot of you probably don't think you can win today. A lot of you don't think you can beat the Celtics. I want each of you to close your eyes and listen." And they did.

"When I was nine years old [growing up in Schenectady, New York]," I said to the players, "my dad told my brothers, Lee and Lenny, to take me down to Lincoln Heights and get me involved in the basketball games. They would throw me into a game, and I would get pushed and shoved. Day after day, I ran home crying and hid in the garage. I didn't want anything to do with basketball.

"This went on for two or three weeks. One night, I didn't come to the dinner table, so my dad got up and walked out to the garage, where he found me hunkered down in a corner. He picked me up, put his arm around me, and walked me into the kitchen. My brother Lee was upset with him. 'Why do you make us take him down there? He doesn't want to play. He's too young.'

"My father stood up and, staring at Lee, said, 'I want you to take him there because I want you to teach him not to be afraid, that there should be no fear. Teach him that competition brings out the very best and the very worst in us. Right now, it's bringing out the worst, but if he sticks with it, it's going to bring out the best.' He then looked at his nine-year-old, teary-eyed son and said, 'Pat, you have to go back there.'"

And I told the players, "I thought I was never going to be able to get over being hurt and afraid. But eventually I did get over it."

As I was talking, I was slowly pacing back and forth, staring at the ceiling, locked into the image of my father's face. Looking at the players, I saw that Michael Cooper, one of our stars, was crying. A couple of other guys looked as if they were about to start.

"I don't know what it's going to take for us to win tonight," I said. "But I do believe that we're going to go out there like warriors, and that would make our fathers proud."

We won the game. I never had any fears about losing. We also won three of the next four games. And the 1985 championship became ours. Seven times in Laker history, the NBA finals had been lost to those adversaries. Now the Celtic Myth was slain, and the choke image with it. . . .

People are products of their environments. A lucky few are born into situations in which positive messages abound. Others grow up hearing messages of fear and failure, which they must block out so the positive can be heard. But the positive and courageous voice will always emerge, somewhere, sometime, for all of us. Listen for it, and your breakthroughs will come.[18]

As Pat Riley's story shows, there is tremendous power in words. Spoken or written, words have an incredible power to sear themselves into the human spirit. Here's the story of Rick Apperson, who now lives with his wife and two children in Smithers, British Columbia, where he leads a Salvation Army unit.

SURPRISE IN THE DRAWER

I WAS TEN years old growing up in Gettysburg, Pennsylvania, and we were studying great poets in school. One day we came to Robert Frost's well-known "Fire and Ice." I was fascinated with his imagination, his skillful use of language:

Some say the world will end in fire,
Some say in ice.
From what I've tasted of desire
I hold with those who favor fire. . . .

The teacher wanted us to break the full poem down and write what it meant to us. I did so, and when I got home, I thought, *I wonder if I could write a poem myself!* Soon I was scribbling away with a pencil on a piece of lined paper—something about love and flowers and . . . well, it certainly wasn't elegant. But it was a start.

When I showed my little six-line effort to my parents, they were complimentary. The biggest accolade, however, came from my Aunt Mitzie, who happened to be staying with us for a season. "Oh, that's just wonderful, Rick!" she exclaimed.

Enthused by her response, I got another idea: *What if I tried to write a poem for HER?* Before long, I was back with my amateur attempt, which she again praised. "You keep doing that, sweetie," she added. "I love reading your poems!"

So I kept going. Everything I wrote was taken to Aunt Mitzie for review. She kept building me up with each endeavor.

One day several months later, she said, "Would you take this poem up to my room and put it in the middle drawer of my dresser there?" I headed up the stairs. When I opened the drawer, I got the surprise of my life. There in a stack was every poem I had ever given her! She had kept them all. I was taken aback, but I also felt very loved in that moment.

She never said a word to me about her growing collection. But occasionally, I would peek into the drawer to see if they were still there. They always were.

Somehow I think this connects to the fact that right up to the present, I've kept writing poems, devotionals, articles, and other pieces for my blog. My love for the written word has become a big part of who I am and what I do. It all began with a word spoken in love.

"Actions," they say, "speak louder than words." But in a moment, when the divine appointment presents itself, word and deed can combine powerfully. The setting may be unfamiliar; even the language may be foreign. But potent forces are at work nonetheless.

EARS TO HEAR, EYES TO SEE

I WAS ONLY FIFTEEN years old, part of a squirrely missions team from America standing in a pizza parlor in Red Square, downtown Moscow. It was absolutely frigid outside, and I was sipping a cup of hot tea. Not that tea goes all that well with pizza, but I thought maybe it would somehow melt the icicles between my toes.

Across from me stood Sergei Petrochenko, our group's translator. I had felt an immediate connection with him and his adorable young wife, Helen, from the minute we stepped off the plane.

"You have a real knack for languages," Sergei said to me.

"What do you mean?" I asked, surprised.

"I mean you hear the sounds really well, and you repeat them perfectly. You should study Russian. You could come live with Helen and me."

At that moment, a shabby, wild-looking man approached our table. He held out dirt-encrusted hands and mumbled something in Russian. I looked at Sergei, who studied him closely and then gestured toward our unfinished pizza. The man mumbled, *"Spaseeba"* ("Thank you"), grabbed two slices, and quickly exited the building.

I looked curiously back at Sergei, who for a solid week had engrained in all of our heads never to feed someone who came begging.

"Why did you give him food?"

"Because he needed it," Sergei replied matter-of-factly, taking another sip of his tea.

"How did you know?"

"He had Russian eyes," Sergei replied. And that was the end of the conversation.

Fast-forward five years. I was twenty years old and spending a semester in Kiev, Ukraine, with Helen and Sergei studying Russian. It had turned out that Sergei was right about my feel for the nuances of his language. And it was during my four-month stint there that another defining moment came, a direct result of the pizza parlor conversation five years earlier.

I was on a taxi bus when I noticed an old man lying in a busy street. He was close to the sidewalk, but fully on the road. He looked injured. I tossed money at the driver and jumped out, dodging cars as I dashed across the street. I knelt down in front of the man, who smelled of liquor and had a deep gash on his forehead.

"Pomogeetya, Podjalusta," he wept. ("Help me!")

I pulled off my scarf and pressed it to his head as I yelled for help. Unfortunately, people ignored my call. Two younger men laughed as they passed by. I heard one say to the other, "Stupid American. He's drunk."

But as I looked into his eyes, I knew there was more to the story. This wasn't a man who had stumbled in a drunken stupor. He had the "Russian eyes" that Sergei had mentioned. Eyes that conveyed a genuine sense of need, of pain, of desperation. Yes, by the smell I could tell he had been drinking, but somehow I knew that wasn't what caused his fall.

Finally, after what seemed an eternity, someone did stop and offer help. In my broken Russian I told the story as an ambulance drove up to us. They loaded the man into the back and whisked him away . . . I never even knew his name. The man who helped me shook my hand and introduced himself as Pavel. He spoke English.

"The man was robbed. He said he was in the street for much time. Why did you stop?"

I shrugged and offered the only explanation I had. "He had Russian eyes."

Pavel looked at me for a moment, nodded, then turned and walked away.

Today, I live the life of a typical American wife and mom back in St. Louis . . . but because of Sergei Petrochenko's words when I was fifteen, my children are learning Russian, my husband and I are praying about how we might impact Russia as a family, how we can minister to orphans, and whether we should even adopt an orphan. Words can have a powerful and life-altering effect. Sometimes they change a life for the worse, but as in my case, they can also enrich our futures in powerful, even eternal ways.

—KELLI STUART

Seeking Hidden Treasures

My heart is so moved by these stories of hidden talent, secret abilities. They are like gemstones brought to the surface, in a minute, by sensitive, caring people who do not let the moment pass without word-and-deed heroics.

I see this played out daily across the ministry I lead. When in the squalid depths of a Kampala slum Compassion discovers a child with unexplainable math or science genius, I rejoice. But deep within my heart, I am troubled too. Where else are we missing it? What could we do better to discern such talent and ability, seizing the moment to give these children a way to thrive? I wonder which diseases are still killing multiplied thousands because the one person destined to find the cure is trapped in poverty. Malaria? HIV/AIDS? What can be done?

Still, Compassion children who once sat on my lap as very little ones have grown up even in my lifetime to prosper as doctors, judges, scientists, authors, senators, pastors, teachers, and athletes. Very soon one will be elected president of their country.

I draw comfort in the fact that, although, like you, I am only one, I am still one—and so is the very next child I meet. Moment by moment. One by one.

A MOMENT TO AWAKEN THE SPIRIT

How early in life does the spirit of a child begin to fall in love with its Maker? At age twelve? Ten? At the oft-mentioned "age of accountability"?

By now you have figured out that my faith is Christian. Actually, parents of other faith traditions as well as mine have long discovered that the early years are crucial for establishing a child's belief system. *What* is taught may vary, but *when* to teach it is apparent to us all. Children are simply waiting for spiritual guidance.

In fact, their openness shows itself extremely early. I find it interesting what happened when John the Baptist was still *in utero,* several months before he was even born! The Scripture says, "At that time Mary got ready and hurried to a town in the hill country of Judea, where she entered Zechariah's home and greeted Elizabeth. When Elizabeth heard Mary's greeting, the baby leaped in her womb, and Elizabeth was filled with the Holy Spirit" (Luke 1:39–41).

Was this child sensitive to the spiritual importance of what was going on? Hmmm.

Later in the Gospels, we get a much clearer picture of how early a child can respond to God. Jesus had just arrived in Jerusalem to massive crowds waving palm branches and shouting His praises. "But when the chief priests and the teachers of the law saw the wonderful things he did and the children shouting in the temple courts, 'Hosanna to the Son of David,' they were indignant" (Matthew 21:15). They came to Jesus to instill order in the rambunctious little worshipers. Jesus, however, reminded them of the words of a psalm—"From the lips of children and infants you, Lord, have called forth praise." The fuller quotation actually goes like this: "Through the praise of children and infants you have established a stronghold against your enemies, to silence the foe and the avenger" (Psalm 8:2).

Babies and toddlers are powerful weapons in God's hands.

In other words, these little people were *made for this!* They were actual warriors, small but mighty, in the spiritual battle raging over our heads. Their role was to tell Satan to shut up. Okay, to "silence" him is perhaps a nicer way to say it. But either way, babies and toddlers are powerful weapons in God's hands.

A few hours before this confrontation with the religious leaders, some of their compatriots had harassed Jesus about the exuberant praise on His way into the city. He retorted, possibly through gritted teeth, "I tell you, if they keep quiet, the stones will cry out" (Luke 19:40). The Son of God had not the slightest desire to squelch the spiritual expression of children.

I find it interesting that when a group of mothers brought their little ones (the Luke version actually says "babies"—18:15) to Jesus and were shooed away by the self-impressed disciples, He did not correct the situation with "Bring the children to me." He said rather, "*Let* the little children come to me" (18:16). There's a huge difference. By His choice of verb Jesus was indicating that children have a built-in desire to seek Him out. They were created to come His way. They have a hole in their hearts that only He can fill.

I heard a very moving tribute on a special CD in honor of Rev. Billy Graham on his ninetieth birthday a few years ago. I listened tearfully as this grown woman thanked the evangelist for leading her to Christ at a very early age. She said, "When I was a young child, around the age of four, as my mother was sewing at our kitchen table she was watching a televised Billy Graham meeting. I don't remember what he said, but as I watched, I know I was moved by the Holy Spirit of God.

"When the altar call was given, I actually went forward in front of the old black-and-white TV in our living room and prayed to receive Jesus Christ. I have loved and served God since my childhood. I'm now almost forty-eight years old.

"When I hear people question child evangelism, I tell them my story. From that day onward, I knew I would walk with God forever."

If we only attend to children's physical health, diet, education, and self-image, we cheat them terribly. To paraphrase Jesus, what shall it profit a boy or girl if we care for their body, mind, and emotions, yet lose their soul? That is why Compassion International keeps careful track of how many sponsored children around the world welcome Christ into their little hearts. Last year, the total was 152,000. That's more than 400 each day.

We don't want them to have to struggle on their own to find the Savior —the way a little girl named Becky had to do. She's now a grown-up pastor's wife whom I met after she had read *Too Small to Ignore* and it had touched her deeply. She along with her husband, Rick Olmstead, are the driving forces in making Vineyard Church of the Rockies in Fort Collins, Colorado, a place that joyfully welcomes children into its total life.

But all this might never have developed were it not for a "minute" in an evening worship service decades ago, when little Becky simply would not be denied . . .

INVISIBLE

AS I GREW UP in the early 1960s in Southern California, my family's standard practice on church attendance was "every time the doors are open." That included Sunday night services, for sure. Dad, Mom, my older sister, and I were all there, sitting on the hard wooden pews, singing the songs, passing the offering plate, and listening to the sermon . . . until I fell asleep, which happened more than once.

One Sunday night when I was five years old, however, there was excitement when we got home. My sister announced with pride, "Tonight I asked Jesus to come into my heart!" She had taken the initial step of making the faith her own, not just a family tradition.

That's what I want to do, too, I thought to myself. After all, one of my favorite songs was "Jesus Loves Me." I felt that I truly did love the Lord and wanted to be one of His own. But I didn't quite know how to proceed.

My opportunity came a few months later—on another Sunday night—when the pastor neared the end of his message. He moved into a public invitation: "Bow your heads, please. Tonight can be your moment of decision. Tonight you can choose to follow Christ. If that is your desire, raise your hand. . . ." I knew from past experience that he would then call those who responded to come forward for further guidance and prayer.

My heart began to beat faster. This was it! This was my chance! I put up my hand.

The pastor's eyes swept across the little sanctuary. "Anyone? Anyone?" he asked. He didn't see me! Or if he did, maybe he assumed I was too young to know what I was doing. Maybe he thought I was just playing around. I kept my hand up regardless, because I was dead-serious. Maybe one of the other grown-ups nearby would look up and notice me, then come to help me.

The pastor waited . . . waited . . . then finally ended his invitation. "Let's all spend some time kneeling in our pews to seek God in prayer," he said. This was the established format in our church at the close on Sunday night. Afterward, we would all go home.

I was crestfallen. I had wanted, really wanted, to invite Jesus into my heart and life—and nobody would pay attention to me. The raised hand of a little girl had gone totally unnoticed, as if I were invisible.

But as the disappointment subsided, I thought to myself, *So what? I can still kneel here and pray by myself.* If the adults didn't see fit to assist me, I'd talk to God on my own. I wasn't going to give up easily. I turned and crouched down between the wooden pews, as others were doing.

"Dear Jesus, I love You," I prayed with all sincerity. "I want to be

Your child. Please come into my heart." I don't recall what else I said that evening, but I do remember how a physical warmth seemed to rise up through my body in that moment. I knew in my heart that my prayer had been heard. I knew something important had happened.

When we got home, I was excited to tell my sister what I had done. "Becky, that's neat!" she exclaimed. "I'm so glad for you." We joyfully prayed together before we went to sleep that night.

This moment was not forgotten; I continued to follow the path of Jesus as I grew up. By the time I reached college age, I knew what I wanted to study: child development. I would become a teacher of the young.

I also worked as a parks-and-recreation facilitator, enriching the lives of boys and girls. I ended up marrying a pastor, and from the very beginning I worked to include children in the church experience. I determined that what had happened to me that Sunday night as a five-year-old would never be repeated if I could help it. Nobody knew that Jesus was calling a little kid to come follow Him that evening— but He was.

The idea that kids are too young or too distracted to "get it" is a religious falsehood. The Master made time for children. He took their spiritual hunger seriously. So must we.

No wonder this woman not only spearheads children's work at the local level but also was appointed in 2008 to lead a new entity in the Vineyard movement, a National Task Force for Children's Ministry, which sponsors conferences, develops resources, and raises awareness across the country.

I suspect my daughter Jenny must have had a very similar spirit to young Becky Olmstead. One morning when she was about four, we were having a daddy-daughter breakfast at our local McDonald's. We were all alone in the jungle gym slides-and-tunnels portion of the restaurant, except for another father and his young daughter across the room. They were busily talking and eating Egg McMuffins at their little table.

I wanted to get a refill on my coffee, so I asked Jenny to stay put until I returned. When I came back, there she was, dutifully still. But then she announced in a loud, excited voice, "Daddy—they love Jesus, too!"

I didn't quite know what to think. "Who loves Jesus, Jenny?" I inquired.

She pointed across the room to the father and daughter by the slide. I looked over to where her stubby little finger was pointing and met the father's gaze directly. He called back warmly, "Yes, we do. She came over and asked!" By this time, both little girls were beaming.

And so was I, deep in my heart. In that moment I knew my precious daughter was on the right track.

Important Work to Do

It should come as no surprise that God believes in children, trusts them, and uses them for some very important assignments all through biblical history and even today. Whenever a child is mentioned in Scripture, I observe that God is up to something important. In fact, it is sometimes a task too important to entrust to an adult whose cement has long since set. I guess we adults think too much. Maybe we know too much. Probably both: We think we know too much!

One such example of a child being chosen for a very grown-up duty was Samuel. He was a little boy living in the temple under the tutelage of the high priest Eli. This man was a lousy father; I don't know why it was thought he might be a good mentor for young Samuel. But that is how it happened.

Being the high priest, Eli was the one through whom God normally would have been expected to speak. But old Eli's antenna for God was rusty from disuse. One night as Samuel was sleeping not far from the aging high priest, he heard a voice call his name. Thinking it was Eli, the young boy went to him and said, "Yes, can I help you with anything?"

Eli replied, "I didn't call you; go back to bed."

This happened exactly the same way a second time. But on the *third* call, Eli finally got the cobwebs out of his head and realized this might be a divine moment. He told the lad that the next time it happened, he should say, "Speak, Lord, for your servant is listening."

I love what happened next. You would think God would give Samuel—"just a child"—a very childlike, gentle message, such as "Go tell Eli that I love him. Tell his sons to be good."

No, God seized the moment to speak stunningly through a mere lad. He needed a clear, pure channel for this powerful message: "Eli, you're fired! You and your wicked sons are finished in the priesthood!" This was basically the high priest's "pink slip." And God entrusted it to be delivered by a little boy.

Samuel went on to be a great prophet. He must have remembered that God can use a child, because years later when he was sent to Jesse's house to anoint the next king of Israel, he and God kept turning down all the big, strong, tall, impressive sons. Samuel kept pressing. "Are these all the sons you have?" (1 Samuel 16:11). Jesse admitted there was still his youngest, whom he hadn't bothered to present because he was out shepherding sheep and besides . . . he was only a child. That's all Samuel needed to hear.

God does that kind of thing. He uses "only a child" all the time. Sure enough, when David came in, slingshot over his shoulder, smelling of sheep and outdoors, Samuel recognized that he was God's chosen one for the throne. The greatest king ever.

This story lives on to this very day. Hear what happened early on to my friend Bill Hybels, now one of America's most highly regarded pastors. His Willow Creek Community Church outside Chicago is, at 20,000 people, one of the largest in the country. The Willow Creek Association adds a worldwide network of more than 10,000 churches in thirty-five nations. Here is his "minute" in his own words.

THE BOY WHO LISTENED

I WAS IN SECOND GRADE in a Christian school in my hometown, Kalamazoo, Michigan. Just before recess one morning, the teacher read a Bible story about an old man and a young boy to whom God spoke in the night. The next morning, the boy told the old man what God had said.

The recess bell rang. All my classmates dashed out the door. I sat there glued to my chair (which was highly unusual for me; normally I would have been leading the pack toward the playground).

The teacher walked slowly toward me. "Is anything wrong, Bill?" she quietly asked.

I was almost too choked up to speak. Finally, I got the words out: "Do you think God still speaks to boys?"

She smiled at me. "I believe to the core of my being that God still talks to boys. I think God will talk to anyone, provided that they listen."

She turned away, assuming I would jump up and head on to recess. But I didn't. I was frozen with the thought that God might speak to someone like me.

The teacher went to her desk, pulled out a little piece of paper with a poem on it, and handed it to me. "If you're really interested in what this Bible story talked about, you might want to read this later tonight."

The next morning, I returned to school, and as the Bible story was read this day, I reverted to my normal behavior of watching the clock. The instant the bell rang, I lunged for the door.

The teacher grabbed me by the shirt and said, "Not so fast." I gave out a sigh as everybody else rushed past me. Then it was quiet in the room.

"What did you think of the poem I gave you?" she asked.

"I really liked it."

She raised one eyebrow as she persisted, "Did you even read it?"

"Yeah. In fact, I memorized it."

Now she was really suspicious. "You did not."

"Yes, I did," I insisted.

"Okay, then recite it for me. Tell me what it says, right here."

Steadily, I began:

> *O give me Samuel's ear,*
> *An open ear, O Lord,*
> *Alive and quick to hear*
> *Each whisper of thy Word,*
> *Like him who answered to thy call,*
> *And to obey thee first of all.*

My teacher gasped with surprise. She then put her hand on my shoulder and said, "Bill, you keep listening for God to speak, and I think God's hand will be on your life."

From that day on, I began trying to train my ears to hear the whispers of God.

I know and respect Bill a great deal, and I can tell you with certainty that he still has his ear tuned for the whispers of God. In fact, the title of one of his most recent books is *The Power of a Whisper—Hearing God, Having the Guts to Respond*. It tells fascinating stories of the moments God has spoken to him over the years. But it all began with Samuel's story and the alertness of a Michigan teacher to awaken his heart.

A TALE OF TWO BLUNDERS

I HEARD NOT LONG AGO two nearly identical stories about two different boys in the early twentieth century trying to come close to God—with radically opposite outcomes. Both were young Catholic altar boys assisting their priest during the Mass. Both of them, at a crucial moment, fumbled and dropped the glass cruet of wine—the very blood of Christ, according to Catholic theology. There could hardly be a more serious mistake.

The one boy, named Josip, was serving in his village in Croatia.

As the glass shattered on the stone floor and the wine spilled irretrievably, the priest spun around and slapped him. "Leave the altar and don't come back!" he snapped.

Well . . . that is exactly what the boy did. He never did return to church, in fact. At age eighteen he joined a leftist party, and by twenty-five he was active with the Bolsheviks. Young Josip Broz eventually took on an extra surname—"Tito"—as he led the communist takeover of Yugoslavia. He was a notorious womanizer and ruled as president for decades, severely restricting Christian churches all across the nation.

The other boy, named Peter, committed his faux pas at St. Mary's Cathedral in Peoria, Illinois, in almost exactly the same year. He wrote later: "No atomic explosion can equal the intensity of decibels in the noise and explosive force of a wine cruet falling on a marble floor of a cathedral in the presence of a bishop. I was frightened to death. The celebrant that morning was Bishop John Spalding, and as that glass broke, he looked . . . and with a warm twinkle in his eye, said, 'Someday you will be just as I am.'"

And indeed, young Peter Sheen grew up to join the clergy, starting a popular nighttime radio program in 1930. Then in 1951 he pioneered a television show, *Life Is Worth Living*, that drew as many as 30 million viewers a week and won an Emmy Award. He, too, like Josip, adjusted his name along the way; he decided to borrow his mother's maiden name—and thus became famous as Bishop (later Archbishop) Fulton Sheen, a trailblazer of religious broadcasting. He authored more than fifty books.

What a difference a moment makes in a young person's life.

You, even for a moment, are part of a tapestry of people engaged in the life of any child with whom you have a minute. Others may have hurt them deeply. Some may have neglected them, sending a "you don't matter" message deep into their spirit. We don't have to know all the dynamics that bring us to the present moment. But we must all be faithful to play our part when the moment presents itself.

Notice the orchestration of voices in this young woman's life.

STRAIGHT TALK

EIGHTH GRADE can be a tough time for a girl, especially if you think you're overweight and you're not as cool as the other girls in your class. On top of this, I felt all alone at home; Tracey, my next oldest sister (I'm the youngest of four girls), had just moved out to get married.

I felt very depressed—hated going to school—didn't see how things in my life were ever going to improve. I met with a couple of counselors at school in the small mountain town in western Maryland where I lived. They gave well-meaning advice, but it didn't really seem to help for more than a day or two.

I had a small job working in the school bookstore before classes started each day. One morning I was teary-eyed and talking about my problems to a friend. My homeroom teacher, who also taught me social studies, happened to overhear my lament (probably not for the first time). On this day he looked straight at me and took a big risk by saying, "Young lady, you need to get yourself to church! You're letting other people's opinions affect you too much, and what you need to find out is what God wants in your life."

I was taken aback, of course. Our family was kind of on-again, off-again when it came to church attendance, although Tracey and her new husband had decided, as part of premarital counseling, to get serious about following the Lord. They began picking me up for services.

I went with them every week and even joined the youth group. My depression lifted as I began learning that I had value to God. The teens I met turned out to be true friends. One evening during my freshman year, while watching TV news (the first Gulf War was raging just then), I made my personal decision to be a Christian, asking God to care for me and protect me in this crazy world. It was the start of a whole new life for me.

The following summer, however, I started hanging around with some of the wrong people and skipping church. I felt I could justify it, because I was often babysitting late on Saturday nights, and I needed the money. If I didn't get to bed until two or three in the morning, it was just too hard to get up, I told myself.

Once again, God sent a loving adult to confront me. My youth leader caught me one Sunday morning and said, "Jennifer, I need to speak to you after service. Wait for me in the lobby, okay?"

Uh-oh. I braced myself for a lecture.

When we met after the sermon, she said, "I need to tell you that I'm concerned about you—the times I don't see you here on Sundays, the stories I hear about your choices. You really need to think more carefully about what you're doing."

"Well, wait a minute," I snapped back. "I'm not doing anything wrong. Babysitting provides the money I need, you know? And it upsets me to hear you insinuate that I'm acting out of line."

The woman was just about to reply when Tracey stepped around the corner from the sanctuary—in tears. "I asked her to talk to you," she confessed. "I'm worried about you. I really don't want you to back away from the Lord!"

At that moment, all of the fight left me. My sister, who had often thought I was a little pest, really cared about me. She desperately wanted me to hold to the right path and not mess up my future.

That is what I did. The next year, a new boy named Josh Wilson moved in from Baltimore, and we started dating. We ended up getting married and going off to Asbury University, a Christian college in Kentucky, where we both graduated. Today we have two children and have been involved in leading youth in our church throughout our marriage. We try to "speak the truth in love" (Ephesians 4:15) to the teens, just as was done for us in the past. We know that following Christ faithfully is the best way for a young person to live.

—JENNIFER WILSON

If you think the people in Jennifer's story went out on a limb to correct and guide her spiritual walk, read the next story about a godmother in Paraguay who lovingly and courageously seized her moment—just in time!

BENEDICTION

IT WAS LONELY for me growing up in a poor barrio of Asunción, Paraguay, the odd one of the family. My mother had borne me out of wedlock, but then she had found a common-law husband, and together they had six more children. I didn't quite fit the new picture.

For comfort and affirmation I leaned on the shoulder of my *madrina* (godmother), an older single woman named Agustina Meza. She worked as a tailor, but most of her free time went to helping in our parish church; indeed, she was the priest's right-hand volunteer. Everyone respected her.

From early days I began stopping at her house just to talk. It was she, in fact, who took me at age eight to a different church she had recently begun to attend, where I heard the clear message that God loved me and wanted me as His child. My mother warned me to stay away from this "cult," but I couldn't resist the love I felt there.

By the time I reached my teen years, I was more convinced than ever that my *madrina* was leading me on the right path. She had given me my little New Testament, of which I was very proud. Often I would stay overnight at her house after the Wednesday night prayer meeting, listening to her wisdom.

One Wednesday during the service, she got up to leave early. I followed her out, not knowing why. When we came to her house, she sat me down at the table and then said very seriously, "Lily, I want to talk with you. Open the Word of God to Revelation 2, please. Read verse 10."

I found the place in the Bible and uttered the somber words: "Be faithful, even to the point of death, and I will give you the crown of life."

"Daughter," my godmother continued, "you are like a little chick. You are just getting out of your shell and looking at the big world. You're just now seeing many things for the first time. But the world is a tough place, my daughter. You don't have a daddy. You do have a sovereign Father, though—one who promises so many blessings in this book. I want to tell you something: You will never be alone. It doesn't matter what comes along; He will always be there next to you.

"But God asks something of you: He wants you to keep your heart and mind clean. If you do that, He will take care of you and give you what you desire."

I kept staring at her with wide eyes. This was obviously a very important message she felt she needed to share with me.

But she wasn't finished. "Now open to Deuteronomy chapter 28. This is where your blessings are recited." She made me read the whole long chapter aloud, all sixty-eight verses of Moses' speech to the Israelites, starting with "If you fully obey the Lord your God and carefully follow all his commands I give you today, the Lord your God will set you high above all the nations on earth. All these blessings will come upon you . . ."

When I came to verse 15—"However, if you do not obey the Lord your God . . . all these curses will come upon you and overtake you"—a list of horrors unfolded in vivid detail: hunger, disease, confusion, capture by enemies, all the way to starvation and displacement. The longer I read, the harder I was crying.

I finally got to the end. "Come here," she said, and put me onto her lap. She hugged me tightly—I couldn't remember anyone doing that in my whole life so far. "You are a star in my crown," she said.

"And I want you always, even until the day we are together with Jesus, to stay faithful."

She startled me when she continued, "I am old, my daughter, and I am not going to live that much longer. I love you so much. I won't be here, but your Father will be here for you. Don't be afraid."

I stayed at her house that night and got up early to slip out for school. When I came to my home that afternoon, there was shocking news: Agustina had been found dead of a massive heart attack that morning! I couldn't believe my ears. My precious *madrina* had given me her final words the night before, as if she knew it was her last chance. I would never hear her voice or feel her gentle touch again.

I didn't even get to go to her funeral, because her family came and took her body away to their home area for burial.

The next two years were very lonely for me. I would retreat into the bathroom for my prayer time. I would dream about my god-mother talking with me. During my waking hours I would replay her instructions in my mind. They sustained me through many hard times.

When I was eighteen, I wanted to go to school to become a doctor. My mother, however, said it was too expensive. One of my aunts, who had no children of her own, volunteered to pay instead—if I would return to the traditional church. I could not agree to that, even though it meant giving up my dream. My aunt replied, "Today is the day you stop being family to me."

I told her, "Yes, but I have a Father."

A year went by. The Southern Baptist missionaries opened up a nursing school in connection with their hospital. I went there and, after four years, became a nurse instead.

When I would look at young men who weren't believers, I would almost hear Agustina's voice in my head: *Look at the blessings, and look at the curses!* Eventually I married a Christian man. Sadly, he died in a car accident when our girls were only twelve and seven. But I never had to ask other people for help. As a young widow, I found there was no lack of men who showed an interest in me. Some were okay, some were not and would have taken advantage of me. I said to them all, "My daughters need a Father, not a stepfather. And the Lord will be their Dad."

I am now seventy-seven years old, and my life has turned out very different from what anybody expected. I came to America in my mid-fifties. My godmother's words have been my compass all through my journey. As she promised, this Father has never failed me. I have gone through so many painful things, but He sustains me to this very day.

—LILY FERNANDEZ

A Giving Spirit

Spiritual awakening is almost always accompanied by the blossoming of a generous heart. After all, the Bible says, "We know that we have passed from death to life, because we love each other. . . . If anyone has material possessions and sees a brother or sister in need but has no pity on them, how can the love of God be in that person?" (1 John 3:14, 17). There is something fundamentally wrong with claiming to love God without a passion to love people—some close at hand in your daily life and some a world away.

> **There is something fundamentally wrong with claiming to love God without a passion to love people.**

Katie Keech isn't rich—well, not in money anyway. Yet she remembers her mother's heart both to reach out to children in need and also to speak into her daughter's life about generosity at . . . just the right minute.

You would think Katie would have enough to manage in her busy days and nights as a business major at Texas A&M University. Not many college girls are finding ways to financially sponsor three different children in such faraway places as India and the Philippines, and also carry on a big-sister correspondence with two others.

But the seed was planted more than ten years ago. "I was eight or nine years old," Katie recalls, "and our church was promoting the Operation Christmas Child thing" (the Samaritan's Purse program that sends shoeboxes full of gifts to needy children in December). "My mom and I were shopping at Walmart for our family box, when suddenly I said, 'I want to fill up a box of my own! I can use my allowance money.'"

Katie still remembers the surprised look on her mother's face. She also recalls the words that followed: "You are so generous. You really have a giving heart, honey."

Soon Katie was loading up the cart with a toothbrush, toothpaste, socks, candy, and a few toys, some twenty-five dollars' worth of items altogether. She felt warm inside as she thought about a girl in poverty getting this blessing at Christmastime.

And in fact, "This kind of thing became a pattern for me," Katie reflects. "What my mom said that day was a catalyst. Later on, I bought shoes several times for a shoe drive. When Hurricane Katrina victims started showing up here in Texas, I chipped in to help them resettle.

"And then I saw something on TV about Compassion International sponsorships. 'I want to do that!' I said to myself. Eventually I went to the website and picked out my first little girl. Shortly afterward, I added more. In fact, I'm planning to go visit one of my children in India."

The funding for sponsorship—thirty-eight dollars a month per child— has required that Katie find a part-time job, along with her studies. She doesn't mind the hours at all, she says. "It's such a joy to work for this kind of purpose. It truly is more blessed to give than to receive."

Out of the Flames, a Calling

When I think about my own life, I wish I had an upbeat story of one lofty, inspirational minute to share like these in this chapter. A minute that might explain why I care so deeply about children. A loving example that I follow, a spoken challenge, or a tender compliment that launched a lifetime of defending children and advocating on behalf of those who cannot speak for themselves.

Actually, I do have a story—the story of one minute (to be precise, ninety seconds). But it is not an easy one to tell. It does not come from goodness or kindness that inspired me, but rather from a very dark moment of cruelty. It was the moment when I was at my saddest, most lonely, depressed, hopeless bottom; in fact, I've never been that low since. The cement of my soul was soft and I was easily hurt. Yet I had a rage and courage in me that made that minute the pivotal one of my life. When I survived it, I knew my calling in life. It was my spiritual awakening. My whole life changed that afternoon, when I was ten years old.

There were a million ways to earn a beating in that place.

My moment involved a candle—a pink birthday candle. Sounds nice, I know—but its blunt end had been trimmed with a pocketknife to create a double tool of torture that could burn from both directions. And I was forced to hold it in my trembling fingers as both ends were lit with a match by the man who was in authority over me—the houseparent at my boarding school for missionaries' children (MKs) in Africa.

This school had been my "home" for nine months of each year since I was little. Mission policy in those years dictated that all MKs leave their moms and dads at age six and travel hundreds of miles across Africa—a week by truck—to this isolated school in the jungle. The people in charge were missionaries who had gone to Africa to save souls but didn't measure up linguistically or cross-culturally. So they had instead been assigned to the lowest, least desirable task on the mission field—taking care of other missionaries' children. They were resentful, angry, and unsupervised, and took out their frustration and rage on their most convenient targets—the innocent children in their charge.

All of my young life at this school, I had endured beatings. Belt buckles and truck tire tread sandals had bruised and torn my flesh. There were a million ways to earn a beating in that place—unspeakable infractions like a wrinkle in your bedspread or being caught with your eyes open during naptime.

When I was nine years old, we were taught in math class how to average a set of numbers. The most frequently recurring thing in my life I could think of was how many times they beat me, and for a very sad span of weeks, I kept track, hiding the tally under my pillow. When I did the math, I discovered I was being beaten an average of seventeen times per week.

The staff at this boarding school abused us in every way a child can be abused—not only physically and emotionally, but also spiritually. We children were terrified of their powerful and vengeful God, painfully reminded daily that we were "little sinners."

I won't dwell on the sexual abuse we endured, but anywhere evil reigns unchecked, this favorite weapon of Satan's always lurks. Tragi-

> **We were admonished repeatedly, "If you tell what happens here, you will destroy your parents' ministry in Africa."**

cally, the same people who read us Bible stories and beat us during the day also prowled our dormitory halls at night, preying on the defenseless innocents. Older boys, victims themselves, learned how to mimic their elders in that depraved environment to serve their own lustful desires; they abused the younger children, using blackmail and physical pain to silence us. There was no one to protect us. We had no advocates, no arms to run to. The very people who should have been our trusted defenders were in fact our attackers.

For years, fifty of us little children had courageously maintained our silence. We were admonished repeatedly, "If you tell what happens here, you will destroy your parents' ministry in Africa. They will have to leave the field, and as a result, Africans will burn in hell because of you!" Our abusers used our love for God, our love for our parents, and our love for Africans to secure our silence about the horrors of that place. (In study after study, child psychologists have been stunned to discover the amount of pain and abuse that children are willing to endure to protect those they love.)

Oh, we wrote letters home every Sunday. But we couldn't even hint at our sadness, loneliness, or the abuse. All our letters were censored, and the slightest attempt to cry out to our parents resulted in a beating, and then a forced rewriting of the letter. We learned to be silent, like lambs. We had no idea our silence was enabling the perpetuation of the evil against us.

Even in the three months home with our parents every year, we all kept our silence. We loved them so much. We knew how passionately they spread the gospel, and I loved my African village friends. If my silence about my abuse could win their salvation, I would endure *anything*.

At school, we were not allowed to have pictures of our parents or to cry from homesickness. Each year, my mind would capture the final image of my parents saying good-bye. For the first month, I could see them every time I closed my eyes, and, at the tender ages of six, seven, or eight, I couldn't help but cry myself to sleep every night, as silently as possible.

But by the ninth month of school, I could no longer remember what my parents looked like. I was so afraid I would break their hearts by not recognizing them when I went back home.

Finally . . . after a year on furlough in America, I found myself at New York's Idlewild Airport (now JFK) with other MKs saying good-bye to our parents. We were about to board a propeller plane that would take us back to Africa, while our parents would follow by ship. At the gate, I took my mother's face in my hands and couldn't let go. I stared intently at her beautiful, kind expression.

> **I had done the unthinkable— I had broken the code of silence.**

"What are you doing, Wesley?" she asked.

"Mommy, I just don't want to forget what you look like."

Well . . . that broke her heart. She dissolved into tears, and so did I. I saw a moment of opportunity, a glimmer of hope for rescue. In thirty seconds, I blurted out my desperate plea. "Mommy, please don't send me back! Please don't send me back! They hate me . . . they beat me . . . I'm scared," I begged, crying, "Please, *please*!"

I will never forget the look of horror in my mother's eyes. "What?!" She gasped in shock. She held me tightly. "What . . . what can I do?" I could feel her sobbing in my embrace.

But less than a minute later, the call came to board the plane. My sister and I were whisked away with all the other children. My friends, who had overheard me, stared at me. As far as they were concerned, I was a "dead man walking." They didn't want to be near me for fear of sharing in my punishment, which was sure to come, so they wouldn't even sit with me or talk to me on the two long flights. I had done the unthinkable—I had broken the code of silence. I had *told*.

On the ship during my parents' month-long voyage back to Africa, my brokenhearted and confused mother suffered a major psychological breakdown. When she arrived, she was quickly sent back to America for treatment.

Word of her illness and what had caused it spread like wildfire. When it reached the boarding school, the staff was enraged. This is what caused the houseparent to march me to the school's dining hall, drag a metal chair across the concrete floor, and slam it down in front of all my schoolmates. Then he threw me up on the chair and jammed the candle in my hand. His tirade began:

"Children, you cannot serve both God and Satan. Wesley has tried. You cannot burn a candle at both ends without getting burned. Watch what happens when you try!"

Fifty terrified children stared in silence. Nobody dared to breathe as the man struck a match and lit both wicks of the candle. "Watch!" he ordered.

Standing on that chair, my knees knocking in fear, I stared incredulously at the candle in my shaking fingers. I contemplated what this would mean very soon. I was at my lowest, darkest moment. I cannot describe to you the cumulative hurt, rage, hopelessness, and despair that welled up and wracked my ten-year-old soul. At this man's hand, I had always lost— had always been manipulated, hurt. Plain and simple, he was bigger and stronger—he was a man, I was a boy. So I was resigned to this new level of humiliation . . . why not yet again?

"This little boy standing here is Satan's favorite tool," he declared, turning to his audience. "He *told*, and the Devil used him to destroy his parents' important ministry in Africa. There will be Africans in hell because of this boy, Wesley."

I had been resigned to my coming humiliation. In minutes, I would scream and throw down the candle. Then I heard this last despicable phrase once again. This time it broke my heart more than the humiliation, more than any physical pain that was about to come my way. I loved Africans. In my heart I *was* African. After each nine-month stint of hell at the boarding school, my spirit had been restored by the loving-kindness of the poverty-stricken Africans in my village. They shaped my heart and soul.

> **I was *not* "Satan's tool." I was just a little boy with a broken heart who had found his voice.**

I viewed myself as my dad's right-hand man. We took the gospel to new villages together, where no white man had ever gone before. I shot my slingshot into the trees to keep noisy birds away so my father's voice could be heard as he spoke to audiences. I was a missionary as far as I was concerned, convinced my dad couldn't do his ministry without me.

Suddenly that afternoon, from deep within me arose a strength I cannot fully explain—a rage, a passion. I had felt I could endure almost any treatment at this man's hands. But this time, with the candle, it was different. Never had words cut so deep.

As the flames licked closer to my skin, I had a desperate thought: *I could win this time!* All through the years, I had lost everything to these people. But this time, the headmaster had unwittingly put himself in a place where I could actually *win*, if I was willing to endure enough pain. I knew in my heart that he was wrong. He was lying, and I felt the evil and injustice to the core of my soul.

I was *not* "Satan's tool." I was just a little boy with a broken heart who had found his voice and cried out for rescue. So, *enough!* Enough shame, enough abuse, enough lies. It had to stop somewhere, sometime. I made my decision: *It stops now! I'm not letting go!* Nothing—and I meant *nothing*—was going to make me cry out or drop that candle. Here is where I would take my stand. This would be my little Masada showdown.

I shook violently, tears brimming in anticipation of the pain of my burned flesh. The man's diatribe kept growing in intensity. But I could no longer hear his voice. All I could hear was the pulsing of blood in my ears as my heart pounded wildly. I clenched my teeth, tightened every muscle in my body, and pinched the candle as fiercely as I could. My rage consumed me. I stared as the edges of my fingers turned red. One blister popped up, then another.

The wide eyes of my best friend seemed to implore, *Drop it, Wesley, drop it!* But suddenly, I was transported out of my body. I floated above this terrified little boy on the chair, watching as if it were happening to someone else. I saw a wisp of smoke curl up on either side of my fingers. I would *not* let go, I would *not* let go. . . .

Just then a boy in the front row could stand it no longer. He jumped up and slapped the candle out of my hand. The children scattered in all directions. The meeting was over.

But standing there alone on my chair, I had received my calling. In an instant, I had gone from *victim* to *victor*. I would, from that day forward, protect children! I would forever speak up for those who cannot speak for themselves.

I tell you the story of the candle so you can understand what a watershed event it was in my life. My whole span on this earth can be timelined B.C. (Before Candle) and A.D. (After Damage). God took one of the worst evils a human being could devise and redeemed it as a life commission for me. My spirit was awakened to what God wanted me to do for the rest of my years.

This chapter of our journey together grips my heart. The spiritual nurture of a child is among our most sacred trusts. We can set the course of their future—indeed, their eternity, if we will.

I am convinced that is why Jesus, in Matthew 18:6, spoke His harshest, most graphic words of threat and warning to those who would cause one of these tender, impressionable little ones to stumble—emotionally, physically, sexually, or spiritually. Beside the Sea of Galilee He gritted His teeth and warned that you would be better off with a two-ton millstone rock hung around your neck . . . no, wait, that's not scary enough, AND be thrown into the depths of the sea. Can you imagine the terror of that? Good—it would be a better fate for you than to cause a child to stumble!

If harming a child can evoke such rage in Jesus, doesn't it stand to reason that the opposite, to bless a child, would bring Him His greatest joy? When, in a minute, a child comes to understand His love, I am sure all the hosts of heaven jump to their feet and cheer!

Funny how most of us who believe in heaven often don't live as if we fully expect to spend the vast majority of our existence there. We give it little thought; it barely influences how we live now, what we do with our time, resources, and even relationships. It is just a heartbeat, a breath away at any given moment. Still we live as if it is fiction, a fairy tale, something possibly in the remote future, in the sweet by and by.

When it comes to "making moments" in the lives of children around us, we need to realize that we very likely may not get to witness the full outcome of our moment until we walk into heaven. We may discover that the brief moment we spent with a child put in motion the greatest accomplishment of our lifetimes! When God says, "Well done," we will suddenly realize we did the most significant thing from eternity's perspective in a moment. That spiritual nurturing of a child turned out to be the tiny splash of a pebble in the pond that sent out ripples of blessing for the rest of time, to the very shores of heaven. It will be so clear then, when the dark veil is lifted and we are no longer looking through a "glass darkly." We will then fully appreciate the power of what we did.

Section Six

A MOMENT TO STRETCH THE MIND

What separates human beings from the rest of the animal kingdom? In great measure it is our capacity to reason, to create, to communicate complex thoughts. All of this is made possible by a gooey mass inside our skulls about the size of this morning's bowl of oatmeal. Without a doubt, we are "fearfully and wonderfully made" (Psalm 139:14).

Throughout history we have not always understood how the mind works. But we have still used and abused it in wonderful and terrifying ways. Satan messed with Eve's mind clear back in the garden of Eden as his first tactic to separate people from their Creator, and thus break God's heart. Propaganda and mind control has long been the first wave of attack in historic warfare. It has always proved more powerful than clubs, swords, guns, bombs, missiles, or remotely guided drones.

Today, it is what convinces a teenage boy or girl to strap on explosives, walk into a crowded marketplace, and blow themselves up, along with as many innocent bystanders as possible. In the suicide bomber's mind, it makes perfect sense, or they would never do such a heinous act. The ability to control another's mind drove the Crusaders, the Nazi hatred, the Communist seizure, and today is the driving force behind terrorism. It's also the genius behind advertising that creates "needs" and causes us to fill our homes (and storage units) with stuff we were convinced at one point we couldn't live without.

Amazingly, these forces are very capable of penetrating even the hardest concrete of educated, savvy grown-ups. But what if the "cement" is that of a child—still soft, moist, and easily impressionable? Little spirits attune to what is going on around them. They are constantly asking "Who am I? What matters? How should I behave? What should I do? What is right and what is wrong?"

In a previous section I told the tragic story of how Adolf Hitler's young mind answered those questions and why. As an adult, his mind was filled with resentment, shame, hatred, and an insatiable drive for revenge and domination. That's one reason he started the *Hitler-Jugend* ("Hitler Youth") movement as early as 1922, a full decade before he formally became chancellor of Germany. Its membership grew from 5,000 boys age fourteen to eighteen in 1925 . . . to 25,000 in 1930 . . . to 108,000 when the Nazis took over in early 1933 . . . to 2.3 million by the end of that year (partly by swallowing whole the Lutheran youth movement of 600,000 members). By December 1936, membership was mandatory across the Third Reich. Its stated purpose: to build "Aryan supermen" for the future of the world.

Long before the first shot was fired, or the first Jew was arrested and thrown into a concentration camp or gas chamber, this campaign was teaching German youth to proudly don the Nazi uniform, salute the swastika, and bow to the future Fuehrer's hateful and terrifying agenda. Hitler fully grasped the significance of childhood and the power of masoning "wet cement."

> **It is a rare church that spends more than 15 percent of its budget on ministry to children.**

So did Mao Tse-tung, who set up the Socialist Youth League of China even earlier than Hitler's, in 1920—a year ahead of the actual Communist Party in that nation. Today it is called the Communist Youth League and has spawned a number of party chairmen and general secretaries, including the current Chinese president, Hu Jintao.

Among the League's responsibilities is overseeing the Young Pioneers with their trademark red scarves, a vast movement (130 million members) for children age six through thirteen. Their pledge translates as follows: "I am a member of the Young Pioneers of China. Under the Pioneers flag I promise that: I love the Communist Party of China, I love the motherland, I love the people; I will study well and keep myself fit [literally, exercise well] to prepare for contributing my effort to the cause of communism."

Meanwhile, how well are we shaping the minds and loyalties of young Christians in the West? It is a rare church that spends more than 15 percent of its budget on ministry to children. This reality is what drove me to Compassion International over thirty-four years ago. Children . . . it's all we do.

The cultivation of young minds is central to history, for good or evil. While the overall process is long, the power to influence a child's intelligence can bear fruit in just a minute.

A CLASS OF "RETARDS"

ON MY FIRST DAY of teaching, all my classes were going well. Being a teacher was going to be a cinch, I decided. Then came period seven, the last class of the day.

As I walked toward the room, I heard furniture crash. Rounding the corner, I saw one boy pinning another to the floor. "Listen, you retard!" yelled the one on the bottom. "I don't give a [blank] about your sister!"

"You keep your hands off her, you hear me?" the boy on top threatened.

I drew up my short frame and asked them to stop fighting. Suddenly, fourteen pairs of eyes were riveted on my face. I knew I did not look convincing. Glaring at each other and me, the two boys slowly took their seats. At that moment, the teacher from across the hall stuck his head in the door and shouted at my students to sit down, shut up, and do what I said. I was left feeling powerless.

I tried to teach the lesson I had prepared but was met with a sea of guarded faces. As the class was leaving, I detained the boy who had instigated the fight. I'll call him Mark. "Lady, don't waste your time," he told me. "We're the retards." Then he strolled out of the room.

Dumbstruck, I slumped into my chair and wondered if I should have become a teacher. Was the only cure for problems like this to get out? I told myself I'd suffer for one year, and after my marriage that next summer I'd do something more rewarding.

"They got to you, didn't they?" It was my colleague who had come into my classroom earlier. I nodded.

"Don't worry," he said. "I taught many of them in summer school. There are only fourteen of them, and most won't graduate anyway. Don't waste your time on those kids."

"What do you mean?"

"They live in shacks in the fields. They're migratory labor, pickers' kids. They come to school only when they feel like it. The boy on the floor had pestered Mark's sister while they were picking beans together. I had to tell them to shut up at lunch today. Just keep them busy and quiet. If they cause any trouble, send them to me."

As I gathered my things to go home, I couldn't forget the look on Mark's face as he said, "We're the retards." *Retards.* That word clattered in my brain. I knew I had to do something drastic.

The next afternoon, I asked my colleague not to come into my class again. I needed to handle the kids in my own way. I returned to my room and made eye contact with each student. Then I went to the board and wrote *ECINAJ.*

"That's my first name," I said. "Can you tell me what it is?"

They told me my name was "weird" and that they had never seen it before. I went to the board again and this time wrote *JANICE.* Several of them blurted the word, then gave me a funny look.

"You're right, my name is Janice," I said. "I'm learning-impaired, something called dyslexia. When I began school, I couldn't write my own name correctly. I couldn't spell words, and numbers swam in my head. I was labeled 'retarded.' That's right—I was a 'retard.' I can still hear those awful voices and feel the shame."

"So how'd you become a teacher?" someone asked.

"Because I hate labels, and I'm not stupid, and I love to learn. That's what this class is going to be about. If you like the label 'retard,' then you don't belong here. Change classes. There are no retarded people in this room.

"I'm not going to be easy on you," I continued. "We're going to work and work until you catch up. You *will* graduate, and I hope some of you will go on to college. That's not a joke—it's a promise. I don't *ever* want to hear the word 'retard' in this room again. Do you understand?"

They seemed to sit up a little straighter.

We did work hard, and I soon caught glimpses of promises. Mark, especially, was very bright. I heard him tell a boy in the hall, "This book's really good. We don't read baby books in there." He was holding a copy of *To Kill a Mockingbird.*

Months flew by, and the improvement was wonderful. Then one day Mark said, "But people still think we're stupid 'cause we don't talk right." It was the moment I had been waiting for. Now we could begin an intensive study of grammar, because they wanted it.

I was sorry to see the month of June approach; they wanted to learn so much. All my students knew I was getting married and moving out of state. The students in my last-period class were visibly agitated whenever I mentioned it. I was glad they had become fond of me, but what was wrong? Were they angry I was leaving the school?

On my final day of classes, the principal greeted me as I entered the building. "Will you come with me, please?" he said sternly. "There's a problem with your room." He looked straight ahead as he led me down the hall. *What now?* I wondered.

It was amazing! There were sprays of flowers in each corner, bouquets on the students' desks and filing cabinets, and a huge blanket of flowers lying on my desk. *How could they have done this?*

I wondered. Most of them were so poor that they relied on the school assistance program for warm clothing and decent meals.

I started to cry, and they joined me.

Later I learned how they pulled it off. Mark, who worked in the local flower shop on weekends, had seen orders from several of my other classes. He mentioned them to his classmates. Too proud to ever again wear an insulting label like "poor," Mark had asked the florist for all the "tired" flowers in the shop. Then he called funeral parlors and explained that his class needed flowers for a teacher who was leaving. They agreed to give him bouquets saved after each funeral.

That was not the only tribute they paid me, though. Two years later, all fourteen students graduated, and six earned college scholarships.

Twenty-eight years later, I'm teaching in an academically strong school not too far from where I began my career. I learned that Mark married his college sweetheart and is a successful businessman. And, coincidentally, three years ago Mark's son was in my sophomore honors English class.

Sometimes I laugh when I recall the end of my first day as a teacher. To think I considered quitting to do something *rewarding!*[19]

—JANICE ANDERSON CONNOLLY

The Troublemaker

That story reminds me of something similar in the early life of one of the most beloved Bible teachers and authors of our time, Dr. Howard Hendricks. He was a poor student as a boy, in a poor school system that kept passing him along each year regardless of performance. Each teacher would write a warning in the file that said, "He's not all that bright. He doesn't like school. He doesn't try very hard, and is a 'handful' to manage."

When he arrived in sixth grade, the teacher sat him down right away and said, "Do you know what your teachers have been telling me about you? They say—" The boy sat there fidgeting; he was well aware of his reputation.

Then she stopped and looked straight at him. "But Howie," she said, "I don't believe a word of it!" From that day on, she began to teach him as if he was smart.

This is the man who grew up to write sixteen books, teach at Dallas Theological Seminary for more than fifty years, speak in eighty countries of the world, and serve a stint as chaplain to the Dallas Cowboys football team.

Sometimes along with saying or doing the right thing, the magical ingredient is timing. Here's an example:

NOUNS AND ADVERBS

SEVERAL YEARS AGO, a public school teacher was hired and assigned to visit children who were patients in a large city hospital. Her job was to tutor them so they wouldn't be too far behind when well enough to return to school.

One day, this teacher received a routine assignment to visit a particular child. She took the boy's name, hospital, and room number, and was told by the teacher on the other end of the line, "We're studying nouns and adverbs in class right now. I'd be grateful if you could help him with his homework."

It wasn't until the visiting teacher got outside the boy's room that she realized it was located in the hospital's burn unit. No one had prepared her for what she was about to discover on the other side of the door. Before being allowed to enter, she had to put on a sterile hospital gown and cap because of the possibility of infection. She was told not to touch the boy or his bed. She could stand near but must speak through the mask she had to wear.

When she had finally completed all the preliminary washings and was dressed in the prescribed coverings, she took a deep breath and walked into the room. The young boy, horribly burned, was obviously in great pain. The teacher felt awkward and didn't know what to say, but she had gone too far to turn around and walk out. Finally she was able to stammer out, "I'm the special visiting hospital teacher, and your teacher sent me to help you with your nouns and adverbs." Afterward, she thought it was not one of her more successful tutoring sessions.

The next morning when she returned, one of the nurses on the burn unit asked her, "What did you do to that boy?"

Before she could finish a profusion of apologies, the nurse interrupted her by saying, "You don't understand. We've been worried about him, but ever since you were here yesterday his whole attitude has changed. He's fighting back, responding to treatment . . . it's as though he's decided to live."

The boy himself later explained that he had completely given up hope and felt he was going to die, until he saw that special teacher. Everything had changed with an insight gained by a simple realization. With happy tears in his eyes, the little boy who had been burned so badly expressed it like this: "They wouldn't send a special teacher to work on nouns and adverbs with a dying boy, now, would they?"[20]

Reversing Course

One of my dear friends is Rhae Buckley. He is a sweet-spirited, wise, godly man who serves Compassion as vice president of human resources. He is responsible for the hiring, training, and development of nearly 3,000 staff in twenty-six different countries as well as our headquarters in Colorado Springs. I don't consider any topic thoroughly discussed until I hear from Rhae.

I shudder when I think how close one person came to destroying this great man. Here is his story in his own words.

NOT SO DUMB AFTER ALL

AS A BOY GROWING UP in Champaign, Illinois, I got off to a fast start in school. By third grade I was put on the "gifted" track, learning a ton and moving up quickly. Yes, it pulled me away from some of my neighborhood friends for special classes, but my parents were pleased at my progress.

Then came fifth grade.

When we heard the name of my assigned teacher that summer, my mother said, "Oh, I remember going to school with her." In fact, it came out that this woman had even dated my father once upon a time. So we had several connections.

Quickly, however, I found that what I expected to be a blessing turned out to be a curse. The teacher pulled me out of the "gifted" program the very first week. I wasn't bright enough for it, she said. "In fact, you're about like your dad," she added. "He never even finished high school, you know." (No, I didn't know that; I quickly verified it at home.) "He wasn't smart enough to do the work. You're going to turn out just like him, I imagine."

Obviously, something was still irritating her from the breakup with my father years before. My presence in her classroom was dredging up bad memories. As the weeks went by, I could do nothing right. My grades slipped downward from what I was used to. *Maybe I'm not as smart as I thought,* I murmured to myself. I would compare my work with my classmates', and my output seemed to be equal to theirs. But the grades certainly didn't reflect it.

Maybe this schoolwork stuff isn't for me after all, I wondered. *Perhaps I should just stick to sports and music—which I love—and let the rest slide.*

At home, I began looking at my father in a different light. He was working two and sometimes three jobs to support our family . . . but was that because he couldn't get a real salary to carry the load? Maybe he was more of a loser than I knew. I pulled back from talking to him.

Whenever I brought home a report card, my parents would say, "Are you doing your best? Looks like you need to work harder." I couldn't find the words to tell them that my teacher basically had me pigeonholed. I kept plodding along, thinking that if only I could survive until May, I would be done with her and on to somebody else.

Then came the day when end-of-year report cards were handed out. I opened mine—and was shocked to read at the bottom what felt like a prison sentence: "Student will repeat fifth grade." No! I was heartbroken.

I went home and started spilling to my mother all the unreported trials of the previous year. She tried to comfort me, but I was inconsolable. I was also angry. At one point, in my immaturity, I blurted out, "I don't want to be like Dad! I'm not that dumb!"

It so happened that about that time, my mother's mother came up from Kentucky to visit. I loved my grandma; I had spent many a happy summertime week with her and my grandpa in the past. She was tiny (four-feet-eleven) but powerful in prayer; as far as she was concerned, everyone she met was a potential friend.

As soon as she learned what was going on, she sprang into action. "Rhae, let me tell you something," she said, pulling me close to her face. "You are not dumb! Neither is your father. You are a child of God. He made you; you can do anything in His strength. He will get you through this hard time. I'm telling you the truth! I want you to know that I love you and believe in you. So do your parents." In the background I could hear my mother saying, "That's right!"

Her exhortation struck something deep inside of me. Maybe this teacher was off-base. Maybe I could learn math and history and language and art after all. Maybe my future was not a dead-end street.

My mother asked the school principal for an appointment, at which she said she would not object to my repeating fifth grade (given the fact that I was young for my bracket anyway)—but if I were to spend another year in this woman's classroom, things needed to change. She would have to begin viewing me for what I truly was, not some stereotype.

In the fall, I indeed was placed in her room for a second round. On the first day of school, I was naturally terrified. But her attitude was different this time. She would call on me in class discussions,

SECTION 6 A MOMENT TO STRETCH THE MIND

rather than ignoring me. No more putdowns of my work. No more cynical cracks about my father's intelligence. I wound up with a good learning experience this year, excelling in academics as well as sports. I started learning to play the trombone and sang in the school choir.

It was about this time that I began reading the Bible every night on my own. There I saw that my grandmother had been right. God truly loved me, and that was all that mattered. I needed to put my trust in Him alone, ignoring the negative voices around me. He would carry me through.

Grandma's "Very Good" Reader

Grandmothers sometimes have an eye for things that others miss.

The inspiration to write this book actually came from the immediate and enthusiastic responses I received after I described the "Just a Minute" concept in various speeches around the world. In culture after culture, it always rang true. One time in Galveston, Texas, I spoke to several hundred pastors at the annual conference of the Association of Vineyard Churches. At the end, National Director Bert Waggoner, a warm, bigger-than-life man, said, "Wess, I've got one of those minutes."

Reaching out his hand, he caught the arm of a pastor walking by in that crowded auditorium and asked him, "If you had to say three things that describe me, what would you say?" The pastor, obviously a good friend, looked up, thought a second, smiled, and said, "Well, Bert, you are a man of God. You're a dynamic visionary leader. And, let's see . . . oh, I know— you are an avid reader."

"Bingo!" exclaimed Bert. "I love to read—and I can tell you the minute that happened!"

I stood and watched him get a faraway look in his eye . . . he was a little boy again. "My family used to have a devotional time at the table after breakfast every morning," he recounted. "My father would pass the Bible around the table, and we would each read a paragraph or a few verses.

"Once when I was six or seven years old, my grandmother came to visit us. She was a very important person in my life, and so I was excited about this—but also nervous about reading in front of her at breakfast. When my turn came on one particular day, I stumbled through the verses.

"I then passed the Bible on to the next person. However, just at that instant, Grandma spoke up. 'My, Berten, you are a very good reader!' she said. I was surprised.

"Later when she and I went to the grocery store in our small town, the friendly cashier said, 'Is that your grandson?'

"'Oh, yes,' Grandma replied—and then added, 'and I am so proud of the way he reads.' This single affirmation shaped my self-identity in ways she would never know."

Suddenly standing there in the Galveston auditorium, this storyteller was back with me. But his eyes were moist and his voice faltered as he said, "Today I have thousands of books in my office and home. I remember the minute it all began."

From Earliest Days

When we think of cultivating the mind, our thoughts go naturally to school, to the classroom. But by the time we walk trembling into our very first classroom, a great deal of mind cultivation has already been going on. From our earliest moment outside the womb, we have been learning voraciously. First it is informal, a kind of a socialization process as we feel our way along this strange new world, this foreign culture. We observe, we try a lot of things and ideas. "If I touch that, I get burned. I hate that. What if I do it again?" Quickly that lesson is learned and we move on. "What if I cry? What if I beg? What happens if I smile, flatter, pout . . . ?" We quickly figure things out, often with no one teaching us except ourselves.

But in this powerful educational phase, loving intervention in our day-to-day learning can have a powerful lifelong effect—imprints in the fresh cement.

SPILLED MILK

A FAMOUS RESEARCH SCIENTIST was being interviewed by a newspaper reporter, who asked him why he thought he was able to be so much more creative than the average person. What set him so far apart from others?

He responded that, in his opinion, it all came from an experience with his mother that occurred when he was about two years old. He had been trying to remove a bottle of milk from the refrigerator when he lost his grip and it fell, spilling its contents all over the kitchen floor—a veritable sea of milk.

When his mother came into the kitchen, instead of yelling at him, giving him a lecture, or punishing him, she said, "Robert, what a great and wonderful mess you have made! I have rarely seen such a huge puddle of milk. Well, the damage has already been done. Would you like to get down and play in the milk for a few minutes before we clean it up?"

Indeed, he did. After a few minutes, his mother said, "You know, Robert, whenever you make a mess like this, eventually you have to clean it up and restore everything to its proper order. So, how would you like to do that? We could use a sponge, a towel, or a mop. Which would you prefer?" He chose the sponge, and together they cleaned up the milk.

His mother then said, "You know, what we have here is a failed experiment in how to effectively carry a big milk bottle with two tiny hands. Let's go out in the back yard and fill the bottle with water so you can discover a way to carry it without dropping it." The little boy learned that if he grasped the bottle at the top near the lip with both hands, he could carry it without dropping it. What a wonderful lesson!

This renowned scientist then remarked that it was at that moment that he knew he didn't need to be afraid to make mistakes.

Instead, he learned that mistakes were just opportunities for learning something new, which is, after all, what scientific experiments are all about. Even if the experiment "doesn't work," we usually learn something valuable from it.[21]

Mrs. Warren's Car

One of the most amazing motivational speakers on leadership I know is Zig Ziglar, author of twenty-nine books, member of the Speaker Hall of Fame, and a long-time friend of Compassion. I was talking with him on the phone one day about this book concept when he said, "Funny you should call me in my office, because on the wall across from my desk are photographs of my heroes—people who believed in me and took a minute to lift me up and launch the various chapters of my life. There are twenty-six of them!"

I asked him to tell me about one from his early days.

"That's easy," he said. "It's my first-grade teacher in Yazoo City, Mississippi, Mrs. Dement Warren. I personally owe her more than anyone else on the wall, because if she hadn't done what she did, none of the rest of my life of challenging and motivating others ever would have happened.

"We were new in town, having just moved into Yazoo City from the farm after the death of my father. I had not only a young broken heart, but a weak, sickly body. During first grade, I caught nearly all the childhood diseases—mumps, measles, and whooping cough. I missed many days of school and was so far behind in my studies it was damaging my self-confidence. I felt stupid, never raised my hand to answer a question, and avoided eye contact with my teacher. I had missed four months of that first school year and felt like a failure.

"But Mrs. Warren wouldn't let me give up. At least two afternoons a week she would drive past our house after school ended, park at the end of our driveway, and teach me what she had taught in class that day. From the passenger's seat, I began to believe again. I actually knew some answers in class, and whenever I raised my hand, she would call on me to answer. My confidence was restored just before that little flickering flame was about to go out . . . maybe forever.

"I have no doubt I would have failed first grade, had Mrs. Warren not taken it upon herself to rescue me. Turns out, she impacted my entire life through those moments in her car."

In one of Zig's books he adds, "Had I repeated first grade, I would have been drafted out of high school in World War II and probably would never have seen the inside of a college door. As it happened, I was able to graduate with my class, qualify for the Navy's V-5 pilot training program, and get started in college. Without that training, my entire life would have been dramatically different."

Just in Time

School serves up perhaps some of the scariest moments of childhood. Cruelty has its greatest impact in this foreign setting. But so does kindness, encouragement, and challenge. By the time we hit our teens, still in that learning environment, we can start to despair. But there is still hope—if there is a hero around.

A popular speaker named Sandra Aldrich tells about growing up her first six years in deep Appalachia—Harlan County, Kentucky—and then being moved to a small town west of Ann Arbor, Michigan, so her father could find more reliable employment. Girls in her culture weren't expected to go far in school. They frequently dropped out and, in more than a few cases, became teen mothers.

But in one of her books, she writes:

THREE MINUTES

THE SUMMER BEFORE I entered seventh grade, I met Doris Schumacher, a teacher visiting her elderly Aunt Minnie, who lived across the street from my family.

Schoolteachers frightened me because several of mine had ridiculed my Southern speech patterns, so I was immediately intimidated by Doris, too.

But she smiled and said, "Aunt Minnie tells me you're going into junior high this fall. Tell me, what do you like to study?"

I was surprised by her question. I usually heard only "How's school?" from adults.

I managed, "Well, I like to read, and I like history."

She smiled again, and her graying hair seemed like a halo.

"That's wonderful," she said. "I teach eighth-grade English and social studies in Minneapolis. What do you like to read?"

Two direct questions from an adult! Stammering, I told her about the books I had read that past week.

She nodded approvingly. "Good choices," she said. Then as I turned to leave, she added, "I assume that you're nervous about going into junior high. Don't be; you'll do just fine!"

The conversation probably had taken all of three minutes, but by the time I walked across the street and up our front steps, I was determined to be a teacher "just like Doris!"

In the 1950s, none of the women in my extended family had attended college, so my announcement was a bit unsettling to some of the relatives. But I pulled the dream into my heart and, with God's grace and my perseverance, gained the B.A. and M.A. degrees that later gave me fifteen years in a Detroit-area classroom. Later, those same degrees opened the door for me to pursue an editing career and rebuild my life after my husband died.

Doris is ninety-four now, but she has continued to encourage me over the decades. One snowy morning, years ago, as we chatted by phone, she commented about how far I had come since my school days.

"You're a big part of my success," I said. "You gave me the vision to go to college." Then I began telling her about that long-ago three-minute meeting.

She interrupted me. "No, dear," she said. "The first time I met you was when you were fifteen and visiting Aunt Minnie at the hospital after she'd broken her hip."

"Oh, no, Doris," I insisted. "I was twelve. I remember you stood by the oak table in her front room. The morning sun was coming through the lace curtains and falling across your brown and gray sweater that so beautifully matched your hair just beginning to turn gray."

She sighed, then said, "Oh, my dear, I don't remember that at all."

I chuckled. "It's okay, Doris," I said. "That morning only changed my life!"[22]

This kind of uplift can happen even at a distance. I get to see evidence of this all the time in the letters that Compassion sponsors send to their children. One such case is Joshua Obiero, who started life in an African slum. He writes:

NURTURING A DREAM

NOW I AM IN THE CITY of Nijmegen in the Netherlands, at Radboud University, pursuing a master's degree in the molecular mechanisms of disease.

I joined Compassion in 1993 at the age of nine, and my life completely changed. Not only did I receive financial support that took care of my education, food, and school supplies, but I also got the most precious gift, the knowledge of Jesus Christ and His saving grace.

I remember very well the first person ever to tell me I could make something out of my poverty-stricken life. It was my sponsor, Mrs. Beth Bell. I am forever in debt to her. Having lived in a slum all my life, this was the only lifeline that enabled me to dream. Everything else in my environment showed me the impossibility of ever changing my life. All the crime, the hunger, the poverty told me that I couldn't make it. But the encouragement and love I received from my sponsor kept my dreams alive, and nothing could put them off.

When I was young, I thought I wanted to be a mechanical engineer. Then at some point I thought I would be an accountant. But

I ended up taking biochemistry in my undergraduate degree. The beauty in all this is that I had more than one dream. I could become anything I wanted, just as Mrs. Beth wrote to me all those years.

Now I am twenty-five years old, at the point where I am actually living what God had planned for me. I still have the letters I got, and they are precious to me. Those words made a difference in my life, and they still do even after so many years. I hope to become a researcher in the area of malaria; in particular my dream is to be involved in finding a vaccine against this killer disease.

I recently started sponsoring a five-year-old boy from Colombia named Franco. I hope and pray to be to him what Mrs. Beth was to me. He has to be told; he has to hear words of encouragement, words of love, words that will inspire him.

The saying goes, "The mind is a terrible thing to waste." The opposite is surely true as well: "The mind is a delightful thing to nurture." In this section we've seen that happen in the political arena, the classroom, at the breakfast table, or from half a world away. I've had a front-row seat to witness it done poorly and destructively as well as positively and excellently. Nations rise and fall due to it. And it can be achieved over the course of many years, even decades, as academic degrees are collected . . . or in a single minute of breakthrough in the mind and heart of a child.

A MOMENT TO REALIZE ONE'S CALLING

The 1980s TV sitcom *Cheers,* which won twenty-six Emmy Awards, opened up each week with this theme song: "Making your way in the world today takes everything you've got . . ." Millions laughed at the hilarious, pretty much pointless lives of Sam, Diane, Rebecca, Norm, and the other characters gathered each evening in the Cheers tavern. Perched on their bar stools, they had no trouble pontificating about the messed-up world, while always in some sort of life jam of their own making.

But the song lyrics still ring true today, long after the show ended in 1993. They are especially poignant in the case of children, who seek to make their way in a very big and complicated world.

Adults are forever asking kids, "What are you going to be when you grow up?" Many healthy, self-assured children can excitedly tell you—even though their answer will most likely change from week to week, depending on what vocation last caught their eye. "Fireman! . . . No, policeman . . . No, wait, a doctor! Oh, I know—a pilot!" I love the way they so sweetly and innocently express uncertainty but still a sense of confidence that they can grow up to be anything they can imagine.

When I visit one of Compassion's partner churches in a little village, I know we're being successful when I hear the children of the poor express their dreams for the future. They don't start out that way, for sure. When we first find these children and attach them to a sponsor, they are more likely to answer the question with downcast eyes and a soft mumble: "I don't know . . ." What they are really saying is, *How can I know? It wouldn't come true anyway, so why hope? Why dream?*

The harshness of poverty, abuse, or neglect stifles the dreams of the young. But life can be launched, vocations inspired, guidance given, confidence and hope restored . . . in just a minute.

> I know we're being successful when I hear the children of the poor express their dreams for the future.

That is exactly how my spirit was awakened after the flame had all but flickered out. It happened in one sentence, one moment—during my first week back in the United States at age fourteen. My family had just arrived from Africa in New York City aboard the SS *Rotterdam*.

By now you know the boarding-school abuse I had endured for years. I also had lost nearly half of my little village friends to measles, malaria, smallpox, hunger, or snakebite. I had cried myself to sleep hundreds of nights after we buried my childhood buddies. I wept as I lay in my cot many a steamy tropical night. First my eyes filled with tears; then my ears; then they would spill over and soak my pillow. I would eventually drift off to sleep, only to do it again a few days later.

Now stepping off the gangplank, I was a lost soul in this new and very foreign place. I was homesick for my village. I was prepared to endure this land only as long as it took me to get back on a ship and go home. I didn't know American jargon very well. Didn't get the jokes. Didn't have cool clothes to wear. I had been torn from a gentle African village to step a month later into the biggest, most intimidating metropolis known to humanity. I was shell-shocked.

A man was driving us to a church service one of those first days. My father was in the passenger seat, and I sat alone in the back. The driver glanced my way and said the familiar words, "So, Wesley, what do you want to be when you grow up?"

In my confused state, I wasn't sure I knew anything, much less where all this was leading in my life. After a long, awkward pause, my father came to my rescue. "I've been watching Wesley for a long time," he said. "He has seen a lot of pain and a lot of suffering. He has a big heart . . . he loves help-ing people who are hurting."

I remember thinking, *Really? Is that who I am? Is that what mat-ters most to me?* That was the end of the conversation, but not the end of the thought. In fact, it was a beginning for me. It framed a goal that made sense in light of the candle incident four years before, when I had deter-mined not to give in to abuse. Now in this minute, the tapestry got turned over. The knots and tangles from the backside of the needlework fell into a pattern that suddenly made sense. I was launched!

"He loves to help people who are hurting" rang for years in my heart and mind. Every life option now found meaning and purpose as it was put to the test of "How does it help people? If it doesn't, then is it even worth doing?"

So I couldn't just go to college at Moody Bible Institute; at the same time I also had to open up tutoring programs for children in the nearby Cabrini Green housing project. I wouldn't just get a job; it had to be with the county Juvenile Court. My summers were spent backpacking in the Colorado Rockies with inner-city youths already in deep trouble with the law. After graduation while waiting for the military draft, I couldn't just drive a Chicago taxi; it had to be an ambulance. When my draft notice came, I accepted it so I could "help protect people from Communism." My college coursework and degrees were targeted at helping the poor and oppressed, especially children. Eventually I found my way to Com-passion, where I could pour all my passion into my calling, my purpose, my mission. My father's words echoed through the corridors of my life from that minute forward.

> **To this day I wear my father's ring. It prompts me to remember my calling.**

Years later, at his bedside when he died, I felt my heart just break. I was being left be-hind, with my mission, but without him. Upon his death, I slipped his ring off his finger and placed it on mine. To this day I wear my father's ring. It prompts me to remember my calling and to ask myself, "What can I do in this moment to help people around me, around the world?" Trust me, moments matter—for a lifetime.

The Power of a Father's Touch

As significantly as my own father touched my life and mission, I have discovered that it is often the touch of a father's hand that guides many a child's life into their purpose. Men, you never stand so tall as when you stoop to help a child—especially your own.

Here is the story of a father who, despite the need to get out the door and go to work, stopped to interact with his little son. He could have dismissed this as "a mother's job." But he didn't. The biographer writes:

THE COMPASS

THE GREAT AWAKENINGS that happen in childhood are usually lost to memory. But for [Albert] Einstein, an experience occurred when he was 4 or 5 that would alter his life and be etched forever in his mind—and in the history of science.

He was sick in bed one day, and his father brought him a compass. He later recalled being so excited as he examined its mysterious powers that he trembled and grew cold. The fact that the magnetic needle behaved as if influenced by some hidden force field, rather than through the more familiar mechanical method involving touch or contact, produced a sense of wonder that motivated him throughout his life. "I can still remember—or at least I believe I can remember—that this experience made a deep and lasting impression on me," he wrote on one of the many occasions he recounted this incident. "Something deeply hidden had to be behind things."

. . . After being mesmerized by the compass needle's fealty to an unseen field, Einstein would develop a lifelong devotion to field theories as a way to describe nature.[23]

Sometimes the significant moment at a father's hand costs very little, like the compass given to little Albert. But sometimes the moment costs the father much more. Such was this dramatic moment:

ULTIMATE SACRIFICE

JOKES ABOUT CLUMSY LAWYERS have been around for a long time. But you didn't crack jokes back in the 1930s about the ace lawyer of Chicago mafia boss, Al Capone—he was too good at his trade. Whatever indictment or accusation the feds thought they might pin on Capone, his lawyer could get him out of it. That's why he was known as "Easy Eddie."

Capone trusted Eddie enough to put his entire dog-racing operation in his hands. He had ways of rigging the races that the smartest bettors couldn't figure out. As a result, money kept pouring in to the Mob's coffers.

But then one day . . . Easy Eddie requested an appointment with the cops. "Got something I'd like to discuss with you," he said. The police and FBI agents were wary, of course.

On the appointed day, the man began sharing information . . . naming names . . . explaining activities that had mystified the authorities for years. They got out their notepads and began jotting notes at a furious pace. Their guest kept talking.

Finally, one agent could no longer hold his curiosity. "Thanks very much, Eddie. This is helpful. But . . . why are you sharing this with us? What's the angle here?"

The man's face grew clouded. "I have a son," he began softly. "He's still in grade school. We call him 'Butch.' And . . . I care about him." Eddie paused.

Then he continued, "As long as I stay in this line of work—Butch will have to do the same when he grows up. There's no other way for him. For him to have even a chance at making something good of his life, I've got to open the door now."

Easy Eddie knew there would be consequences to pay for ratting on the Mob. A few years later, Capone's men spotted him driving his car and silenced him forever. Two shotgun blasts did the job.

Meanwhile, Butch grew up to finish high school and, with a cleansed family record, got accepted into the Naval Academy at Annapolis. In the late afternoon of February 20, 1942, he became one of the nation's most heroic fighter pilots, downing three Japanese bombers and damaging two others with only thirty-four seconds' worth of ammunition. No wonder he was awarded the Congressional Medal of Honor. A year and a half later, he went missing in action over the Pacific, and his body was never recovered.

After the war ended, Chicago decided to grant its famous son a local honor. The growing airfield on the northwest side of town would be renamed . . . O'Hare International Airport. The next time you fly through there, stop for a minute in Terminal 2 to see an F4F-3 Wildcat plane along with a tribute to its brave pilot, Butch O'Hare—and give thanks for a dad who paid the ultimate price to free his son's future.

Passing the Pen

Other fathers teach their offspring what they know, setting them up to excel. My dear friend Glen Keane is a leading animator for Walt Disney Studios. In a brilliant career spanning thirty-seven years, Glen has been the creative genius whose heart, mind, and hand have drawn some of the most lovable Disney characters of all time. Ariel from *The Little Mermaid* was his creation, inspired by his lovely wife. And who can forget the beast in *Beauty and the Beast*? That was Glen's work, as were Aladdin, Pocahontas, Tarzan, and most recently Rapunzel in Disney's animated movie *Tangled*.

Glen's father is Bil Keane, perhaps best remembered for his famous cartoon series "The Family Circus." Glen, as a matter of fact, was the inspiration for little Billy in those cartoons. Although with five children at home, it was the real-life family circus that gave Bil his wealth of warmhearted material.

To actually get his daily cartoon drawn, he had to build an attached studio to the family home. He would retreat there to a huge curved desk with a lighted glass top. When Daddy was working, the children knew not to disturb him unless it was really important.

Little Glen adored his father and wanted more than anything to draw like him. He would sit in his little bedroom sketching, erasing, and sketching again to hone his craft just like his dad. One day when Glen was seven years old, he was trying his best to draw a picture of a horse. Try as he may, it kept looking more like a dog. As the frustration grew, he felt he had a crisis worthy of a trip to his father's studio for rescue. He knocked timidly on the door.

"Come in!" came the deep, crisp, commanding voice of Bil Keane. There sat his father at his huge drawing board. Behind him was a world map with colored pins marking the twelve hundred cities that at that time carried "The Family Circus" in their newspapers. Books of all sizes lined the shelves around him. Bil was deep into his work, bearing down on the next important deadline.

Timidly little Glen walked across the studio, reached up, and placed his sketch on the desktop before his father.

"Daddy, I'm trying to draw a horse—but it keeps looking like a dog," he said with a sigh of exasperation. "I've tried and tried to figure it out for myself, but I'm just stuck."

Then came the minute. "Well, let's just take a look at what you've got," his father said. And with a grand sweep of his arm that Glen can still see vividly to this day, his father pushed all of his supplies and sketches off to one side of his desk.

Together they got down the World Book Encyclopedia and looked up horses. "Now just because you're an artist doesn't mean you can draw a horse," his father exhorted. "You've got to study and think about a horse!" Placing a blank sheet of drawing paper over his son's work on the light table, he began explaining. Flipping back and forth from his son's drawing to his own, the magic happened. And right before his eyes, "a horse emerged from my dog," Glen says. He can barely describe the process of those precious moments without a lump in his throat all these years later.

In that moment Glen felt loved and respected. But he also learned that you don't just become a great artist because you "wish upon a star," to quote a Disney tune. It is done with study, hard work, heart, soul, and passion. Still, for the first time Glen Keane realized that it could happen. He could one day be a great artist like his dad. The cartoonist's pen was being passed from father to son.

And all of us who love the magic of Disney animations get to reap the harvest.

Some through the Fire, Some through the Flood

While a life vocation can be crystallized by a moment of kindness, love, and encouragement, it can also be born in painful experiences. It's a sad reality that some of our greatest moral leaders came to realize their calling through a stinging moment. They feel the pain afresh every time they think about it, and it drives their determination to bring change.

Nelson Mandela, tireless crusader for racial justice in South Africa and winner of the Nobel Peace Prize, remembers a telling moment back in 1934 when he and his group of peers were only sixteen years old. Apartheid was of course the law of the land. In his book *Long Walk to Freedom,* he describes the elaborate ceremony that followed their circumcision. They received gifts (two heifers and four sheep, in Nelson's case) and congratulations for enduring the pain and now entering the world of men.

THE CHIEF'S SPEECH

THE MAIN SPEAKER of the day was Chief Meligqili, the son of Dalindyebo, and after listening to him, my gaily colored dreams suddenly darkened. He began conventionally, remarking on how fine it was that we were continuing a tradition that had been going on for as long as anyone could remember. Then he turned to us and his tone suddenly changed. "There sit our sons," he said, "young, healthy, and handsome, the flower of the Xhosa tribe, the pride of our nation. We have just circumcised them in a ritual that promises them manhood, but I am here to tell you that it is an empty, illusory promise, a promise that can never be fulfilled.

"For we Xhosas, and all black South Africans, are a conquered people. We are slaves in our own country. We are tenants on our own soil. We have no strength, no power, no control over our own destiny in the land of our birth. They will go to cities where they will live in shacks and drink cheap alcohol all because we have no land to give them where they could prosper and multiply. They will cough their lungs out deep in the bowels of the white man's mines, destroying their health, never seeing the sun, so that the white man can live a life of unequaled prosperity.

"Among these young men are chiefs who will never rule because we have no power to govern ourselves; soldiers who will never fight for we have no weapons to fight with; scholars who will never teach because we have no place for them to study. The abilities, the intelligence, the promise of these young men will be squandered in their attempt to eke out a living doing the simplest, most mindless chores for the white man. These gifts today are naught, for we cannot give them the greatest gift of all, which is freedom and independence.

"I well know that Qamata [the Xhosa god] is all-seeing and never sleeps, but I have a suspicion that Qamata may in fact be dozing. If this is the case, the sooner I die the better because then I can meet him and shake him awake and tell him that the children of [the great pre-colonial king] Ngubengcuka, the flower of the Xhosa nation, are dying."

The audience had become more and more quiet as Chief Meligqili spoke and, I think, more and more angry. No one wanted to hear the words that he spoke that day. I know that I myself did not want to hear them. I was cross rather than aroused by the chief's remarks, dismissing his words as the abusive comments of an ignorant man who was unable to appreciate the value of the education and benefits that the white man had brought to our country. At the time, I looked on the white man not as an oppressor but as a benefactor, and I thought the chief was enormously ungrateful. This upstart chief was ruining my day, spoiling the proud feeling with wrongheaded remarks.

But without exactly understanding why, his words soon began to work in me. He had planted a seed, and though I let that seed lie dormant for a long season, it eventually began to grow. Later, I realized that the ignorant man that day was not the chief but myself.[25]4

Meanwhile all the way across the world and in about that same era, another future Nobel Peace Prize honoree was undergoing a hurtful imprint upon the fresh cement of his spirit. His name was Martin Luther King Jr.

THE SHOE STORE

I REMEMBER A TRIP to a downtown [Atlanta] shoe store with Father when I was still small. We had sat down in the first empty seats at the front of the store. A young white clerk came up and murmured politely:

"I'll be happy to serve you if you'll just move to those seats in the rear."

My father answered, "There's nothing wrong with these seats. We're quite comfortable here."

"Sorry," said the clerk, "but you'll have to move."

"We'll either buy shoes sitting here," my father retorted, "or we won't buy shoes at all." Whereupon he took me by the hand and walked out of the store. This was the first time I had ever seen my father so angry. I still remember walking down the street beside him as he muttered, "I don't care how long I have to live with this system. I will never accept it."[25]

All my life, as both an African and an American, I have admired Nelson Mandela and Martin Luther King Jr. from afar. I know from my work with impoverished children that at the very root of poverty, beneath the appalling circumstances, is tragic injustice. It suppresses the human spirit, sapping it of joy and the hope that life could ever be worth living, ever be different. It infuriates me!

But this next story is about a very close friend of mine who bridles his fury and, as a result, is bringing peace and justice in one of the most challenging places on earth. He is not as well-known as the previous two civil rights leaders—not yet. But he is, in my opinion, the Martin Luther King of the Middle East. His vision is for change in one of the historic hotbeds of hatred: the Israeli/Palestinian conflict.

With great love, warmth, humor, and courage, Sami and his band of activists regularly put their lives on the line. They disarm both factions at the very points of tension, with surprising love for both. The dignity and humanity of both Israeli and Palestinian is delicately preserved. Tempers cool in these face-to-face encounters.

One day in Hebron, which is a tense flashpoint of this conflict, I sat down with Sami in a sidewalk cafe and asked him why he does what he does. He told me the most amazing moment from when he was a young lad, just twelve years old.

THE OLIVE SEEDLING

IT WAS A JOYOUS ATMOSPHERE on a beautiful spring day in 1984 when we all met at the bus. Dozens of us, Palestinians, Israelis, and internationals, all gathered at the Palestinian Center for the Study of Nonviolence in East Jerusalem. Tensions were quickly rising as Jewish settlers were taking ancient land away from Palestinian peasants in the town of Tiquwa, southeast of Bethlehem.

It was an old Israeli tactic to suddenly, overnight, put up a makeshift fence around a family's farm and claim it as unused, empty land—available to be "settled." Without proper "paperwork" the peasant family had just one recourse, and that was to throw itself on the mercy of the court, which operated with secret files not even their own lawyers could see. And so the family never got justice in the courtroom.

Our counterstrategy was to move in quickly and plant trees on the land, thus confirming its proper ownership and use for agricultural purposes. If it was in such use, the old laws said it could not be taken away from its Palestinian owners. Of course this required knowing which properties were about to be seized, and then beating the fences, settlers, and soldiers to the punch.

So that day's protest was to plant olive trees. Olive trees thrive in that hot dusty environment, but the irony of the olive branch being the symbol for peace made it even more special and strategic. My Uncle Mubarak was the director of the center, and the villagers, in desperation, asked him to help protect their land. I had heard of such courageous and righteous actions around our dinner table. Now I had pleaded to get to go and be part of this adventure. Trusting Uncle Mubarak, my parents said I could.

On this morning, my uncle and other elders explained that it was their job to discuss with the soldiers and settlers. Our role was to quietly plant olive trees as quickly as possible.

Off in the distance, we could soon see the dust billowing up from the rapidly approaching military vehicles. The rumble grew louder; my heart pounded.

Finally, brakes screeched, dust swirled, and they slammed to a stop just feet away from where I was nervously planting a small two-foot seedling.

The captain was angrily shouting. Soldiers fanned out to block our work. I worried for my uncle as he courageously stood his ground explaining the injustice. The elders quietly told us, "Keep planting your trees. . . ."

With my shovel I dug a small hole in the dusty, rocky soil. I selected just the right little tree, small but with strong branches, its roots packed in a black plastic bag. It was the future—I could imagine it big and flourishing one day, holding the soil, providing shade in the dry shimmering heat as well as delicious olives that would be food for the family.

Slowly and gently I placed it in the hole and began putting handfuls of soil around it. I separated out any rocks that might hinder the growth of its roots. Finally, I patted the last soil in place and sat back to admire my work. I had become deaf to the shouting and hassle around me as I cared lovingly for my young tree.

Suddenly a shadow came up from behind me. I felt a presence . . . and watched a uniformed arm stretch over my shoulder, grab my little tree, and, in a split second, yank it from the ground. The arm then hurled it onto a nearby pile of rocks. I can see it today just lying there, roots bare, baking in the sun. Time mysteriously stood still. . . .

I squinted up into the sun and saw the face of the heavily armed Israeli soldier with a smile, a triumphant smirk. He turned and walked away.

Amazingly, the emotion that swept over me was not anger or revenge, but confusion—why would he do such a thing? That feeling was quickly followed by sorrow. I felt sad for my little tree and all it represented. I felt sad for me trying to do the right thing. But mostly, I grieved for the soldier. How sad to be able to do such a thing and then smile about it.

Then I did something courageous. I walked over to my fallen seedling, forlorn on its stones. I brushed the dust from its little twig branches, joyful that none had actually snapped in the violence. I quietly replanted that little tree right back in the same spot. Now from deep within me rose a new emotion—victory!

In the ensuing decades I have planted many such trees. But I will never forget that boyhood moment when I found myself, my purpose, my calling . . . my mission.

After hearing this amazing story, I asked Sami a penetrating question. "If you could go back and kneel beside that young boy and his seedling, what would you say to him?"

He replied, "I would tell him, 'Thank you. Your spirit just launched a thousand acts of love.'" That is because Sami Awad went on to become the founder and executive director of a Palestinian organization called the Holy Land Trust (www.holylandtrust.org). His blog (http://samiawad. wordpress.com) is headlined "Never Give Up." He has dedicated himself to learning and educating others in nonviolence, which is making him one of the leaders of the Palestinian nonviolence movement.

The Dashing of Dreams—in Just a Minute

However, not every child bounces back like these. Some children find their dreams dashed permanently. Whether the act is deviously intentional or inadvertent in a thoughtless moment, it's all the same to the soft spirit of a child.

I once heard of a very skilled veterinary surgeon whose little boy adored him and dreamed of one day following in his steps. At the dinner table one evening, a guest asked the boy if he was going to grow up to be a surgeon just like his father. As he took in a breath to enthusiastically reply, his father's voice beat him to the moment, "Oh, no—he doesn't have a surgeon's hands. They're going to be way too big." In a minute, a dream was squelched.

Something far more premeditated took place in the life of young Alfred Hitchcock. Starting out as a practical joke, his "minute" actually took ten minutes, but one would have been enough. As a result of this moment in a little boy's life, many of us have spent restless nights, with the sheets pulled up tightly to our necks!

Just Kidding Around?

Little Alfred grew up in London, the son of a prosperous importer with many connections throughout the city. One day when the boy was around five years old, his father sent him on an errand. He was handed a sealed envelope and told to take it to the police station nearby. "The captain will read it and then give you his answer," his father said.

Alfred did as he was instructed. He felt proud that his daddy had entrusted him with such a job. He found his way into the building and handed the envelope to the officer in an imposing blue uniform. The man opened the envelope and read the note. He smiled . . . then looked perplexed . . . then smiled again.

"Come along; I need to show you something," he said to the boy at last.

Little Alfred followed the man through a series of hallways and doors until they came to an empty jail cell. Soon the officer was guiding the boy into the cell—and suddenly locked the door behind him.

Alfred looked up, bewildered. As the man walked away, he said, "This is how we handle boys who cause trouble." Nothing more.

Alfred looked around at the cold metal bars. He pushed on the door, to no avail. He realized he was trapped. How would he ever get home again? Soon he began to cry, whimpering at first, then gradually wailing loudly as his panic grew.

Ten minutes passed, by which time the boy was shrieking in terror. Then the police chief returned to unlock the door and set him free. No explanation was given.

Those who knew Alfred Hitchcock from that time onward said that he took on a fearful personality, often seized by trepidations. As a teenager, he had few friends. The strict school he attended, which did not hesitate to use spankings, made him all the more nervous.

He was afraid of heights. Naturally, he did his best to avoid policemen. He always seemed to be on edge.

He worked out his tension as an adult by dreaming up ways to frighten the rest of us, using the silver screen. He became masterful at his craft, winning multiple Emmy and Oscar nominations for such thrillers as *Psycho* and *Dial M for Murder*. His star appears on the Hollywood Walk of Fame. But he never did find out why his father had thought it would be neat to scare him so traumatically. It remained a mystery, a wound in his memory, all the way until he died at the age of eighty.

The Building of Dreams—Also in Just a Minute

Okay, enough negativity. I'm depressing myself! Dreams can also be built for good in a short amount of time. For example, consider this next story by Connie Fortunato:

BIG PLANS FOR A SMALL GIRL

SOME PEOPLE FEEL SORRY for the children of ministers, who must endure constant review by the congregation—"fishbowl living," it's called. But there are advantages as well. When I was growing up, the middle of three children in a Pittsburgh parsonage, we got to meet some fascinating guests. (In those days, most churches would never think of spending money to put a visiting speaker in a hotel; the pastor's home would do fine, it was assumed.)

And that's how I got to sit at the same dining room table with Morris Plotts. He was a giant of a man, at least six-foot-four, and wore a size 16 shoe. No wonder the East African friends he had made on his many missionary trips had given him the playful nickname *Bwana Tembo* (in Swahili, "Lord Elephant"). He had a booming voice, a hearty laugh, and was always telling the most amazing stories.

During one meal when I was maybe seven years old, he turned my way and asked the common question, "And what do you want to be when you grow up, Connie?"

I was too young to have an informed ambition, so I don't remember how I answered. Given the setting, it was probably something about missionary service.

"Well," Morris Plotts responded with his trademark enthusiasm, "if God is in your plans, make them BIG!"

The sentence began to echo in my young mind. I sat there nodding my head, wondering what great thing I might do for God someday. Before Morris Plotts left our home the next morning, he signed our family guestbook that always rested on an end table in the living room. There, beside his name, was his maxim once again: *If God is in your plans, make them BIG!*

All through the years, that sentence has shaped the way I think, the risks I take, the courage I find to keep going when the chips are down. It has pushed me forward to pursue a double major in college (music and literature), to create a music education curriculum for preschoolers through adults, and now to build an organization that brings the healing power of music to orphans and other disadvantaged children across Romania and Ukraine.

When I stand on the podium of a Romanian cathedral or the Philharmonic Concert Hall in Kiev and look into the shining faces of a hundred or more children singing Handel or Mozart, I marvel at what they have learned in just a weeklong camp. Accompanied by a professional symphony orchestra, they astound their audiences with the God-given talents so recently unearthed. Sometimes I close my eyes and, once again, see that page in my parents' guestbook, with its strong masculine handwriting. *Make BIG plans,* I tell myself. *You serve a big God, for whom nothing is out of reach.*

Connie Fortunato is the founder and president of Music Camp International (www.musiccampinternational.org), which seeks to spread music education to children in countries that have traditionally limited these opportunities to an elite few. She has also been a guest conductor and clinician for choral festivals as well as served as an adjunct professor at both the undergraduate and graduate level. She and her husband, Jim, are the parents of two grown children.

As the father of two beautiful daughters, I've always tried to help them know that they can dream big and become absolutely anything they can dream. Here's one teacher who missed her chance—and another who really captured the power of a moment.

WIND BENEATH HER WINGS

IN 1959, WHEN JEAN HARPER was in the third grade, her teacher gave the class an assignment to write a report on what they wanted to be when they grew up. Jean's father was a crop duster in the little farming community in Northern California where she was raised, and Jean was totally captivated by airplanes and flying. She poured her heart into the report and included all of her dreams; she wanted to crop-dust, make parachute jumps, seed clouds, and be an airline pilot.

Her paper came back with an "F" on it. The teacher told her it was a "fairy tale" and that none of the occupations she listed were women's jobs.

Jean was crushed. She showed her father the paper, and he told her that of course she could become a pilot. "Look at Amelia Earhart," he said. "That teacher doesn't know what she's talking about."

But as the years went by, Jean was beaten down by the discouragement and negativity she encountered whenever she talked about her career—until she met Mrs. Dorothy Slaton.

Mrs. Slaton was an uncompromising, demanding English teacher with high standards and a low tolerance for excuses. She expected her students to behave like the responsible adults they would have to be to succeed in the real world after graduation. Jean, now a senior, was scared of her at first but grew to respect her firmness and fairness.

One day Mrs. Slaton gave the class an assignment. "What do you think you'll be doing ten years from now?" Jean thought about the assignment. Pilot? No way. Flight attendant? I'm not pretty enough—they'd never accept me. Wife? What guy would want me? Waitress? I could do *that*. That felt safe, so she wrote it down.

Two weeks later, the teacher handed back the assignments, face down on each desk, and asked this question: "If you had unlimited finances, unlimited access to the finest schools, unlimited talent and abilities, what would you do?" Jean felt a rush of the old enthusiasm, and with excitement she wrote down all of her dreams. When the students stopped writing, the teacher asked, "How many students wrote the same thing on both sides of the paper?" Not one hand went up.

The next thing that Mrs. Slaton said changed the course of Jean's life. The teacher leaned forward over her desk and said, "I have a little secret for you all. You *do* have unlimited abilities and talents. You *do* have access to the finest schools, and you *can* arrange unlimited finances if you want something badly enough. This is it! When you leave school, if you don't go for your dreams, *no one* will do it for you. You can have what you want if you want it enough."

The hurt and fear of years of discouragement crumbled in the face of the truth of what Mrs. Slaton had said. Jean felt exhilarated and a little scared. She stayed after class and went up to the teacher's desk. Jean thanked Mrs. Slaton and told her about her dream of becoming a pilot. Mrs. Slaton half rose and slapped the desk top. "Then do it!" she said.

So Jean did. It didn't happen overnight. It took ten years of hard work, but eventually she overcame opposition and outright hostility to become a private pilot. She also qualified to fly air freight and even commuter planes, but always as a copilot. Her employers were openly hesitant about promoting her—because she was a woman. Even her father advised her to try something else. "It's impossible," he said. "Stop banging your head against the wall!"

But Jean answered, "Dad, I disagree. I believe that things are going to change, and I want to be at the head of the pack when they do."

Jean went on to do everything her third-grade teacher said was a fairy tale—she did some crop-dusting, made a few hundred parachute jumps, and even seeded clouds for a summer season as a weather modification pilot. In 1978, she become one of the first three female pilot trainees ever accepted by United Air Lines and one of only fifty women airline pilots in the nation at the time. In time she became a Boeing 737 captain for United.

It was the power of one well-placed positive word, one spark of encouragement from a woman Jean respected, that gave an uncertain young girl the strength and faith to pursue her dream. Today Jean says, "I chose to believe her."[26]

—CAROL KLINE with JEAN HARPER

So we see that even "failure" in the hands of a "just a minute" teacher can become triumph. I can identify with this next story's math fiasco. To this day I sometimes wake up in a sweat from math class nightmares. This could have been my story . . . except I never had a tutor like Miss Tobin.

SURPRISE BOX

FIFTH-GRADE MATH was definitely not fun for me. I knew, my teacher knew, and even the other kids knew that I just "didn't get it." Eventually I fell so far behind that the school officials recommended a tutor.

I was embarrassed about all this and went fearfully to my first session with Miss Tobin. She was a tall woman in her forties, with a thick German accent. What would she make me do? What if I couldn't understand what she was saying?

"Hello, Michael," she said with a warm smile. "Before we start working on math, I'd like to get to know you a little. What do you really enjoy?"

Soon she had me talking about the love of my life, which was art. "I really like to draw things," I told her. "It's fun to make pictures."

"Oh, is that so?" Miss Tobin replied. "Next time we meet, why don't you bring me some of your artwork? I'd love to see it!"

Somehow the math drills didn't seem so threatening after that. I brought her my pictures, and each time she encouraged me. We made good progress on the subject of math, too, so that after about a month of tutoring, I was able to pass the tests and keep current with my peers.

On our last day together, Miss Tobin said, "Michael, I'm so proud of what you've accomplished. And I can't wait to see what you do with your art in the years ahead. In fact, I brought you a little present." My eyes grew wide as she lifted up a wrapped gift about twelve inches wide and maybe eighteen inches long. I took it in my hands. It was heavy!

"What is it?" I asked.

"Open it and see!"

I tore off the ribbon and paper . . . and there was a special wooden case filled with art supplies: colored pencils, drawing papers in various shades, even a rainbow of oil pastels. I'd never had such a treasure in my life. "Oh, wow!" I exclaimed. "Thank you!" This woman was a specialist in mathematics—and yet she had tuned into something almost opposite, my love for the world of shapes and colors.

I carried it around at recess that day to show all my friends. "Look what Miss Tobin gave me!" This tutoring thing wasn't so bad after all. At the end of school, I floated home on a cloud. I couldn't wait to show my parents. Soon I was busy making new pictures with all my newly acquired tools. For me, this was sheer joy.

I eventually went on to earn a Bachelor of Fine Arts degree in college, and then worked for twelve years as a freelance graphic designer. The interest spotted by my math tutor became my livelihood, until I decided much later to shift to a different line of work. I will always be grateful for her sensitive eye for the potential inside a fifth-grade boy.

—MICHAEL PATTERSON

This man and his wife now live in Buckley, Washington, with their four daughters, the youngest of whom was adopted from Haiti. They also sponsor nine Compassion children in countries from Peru to Indonesia. In his spare time, Michael continues to enjoy sketching for relaxation, as well as volunteering as a Child Advocate for Compassion International. He has spoken so convincingly on his job about children in poverty that a group of twelve coworkers have banded together to sponsor a medical student in the Dominican Republic as part of Compassion's LDP (Leadership Development Program); the young man will, upon graduation, become a pediatrician.

Michael Patterson is an example of hidden potential that an alert educator spotted. Sometimes, however, you only see part of the picture, and somebody else has to fill in the specifics. That was certainly true when I was a camp counselor during college days and met a junior-high kid named Marshall Shelley.

Ours was Mohican Cabin at Woodbine Ranch just outside Denver. I taught rifle marksmanship that summer, and Marshall could hammer a nail with a .22 rifle at fifty yards. I figured he would hit the mark no matter what he aimed at in life. Well, as it turns out, journalism was his target. Today he is a vice president and editor-in-chief of the church leadership media group at Christianity Today International. Here's his story:

COURSE CORRECTION

YOU KNOW IT'S GOING TO BE a bad day in sophomore English when your gruff, no-nonsense teacher hands back everyone else's graded essays . . . then stares at you as he says, "Mr. Shelley, please see me after class."

The assigned subject had been an expository theme on Nathaniel Hawthorne's famous novel *The Scarlet Letter,* in which a young woman in Puritan-era Boston is humiliated for her adultery. I figured my teacher, Mr. Ridgway, didn't like the tack I had taken in my essay. My father, after all, was a church history professor who knew a thing or two about the Puritans, and I had argued that Hawthorne hadn't treated them fairly, portraying only their harshness in this particular story.

But when I nervously approached Mr. Ridgway's desk at the end of the hour, he surprised me by making no rebuttal to my viewpoint. Instead, he critiqued my writing style.

"Mr. Shelley," he said in his typically direct way, "you couldn't write a descriptive paragraph if your life depended on it." I knew it was true; the effusive prose of the classic novelists, where you took three paragraphs to describe every detail of a particular hay wagon or apple tree, wasn't my thing. "Expository themes are clearly not your forte. You have no sense of eloquence or flair."

I held my breath. Where was this going? Was he giving me an *F?*

He looked me right in the eye as he continued, "But you'd make an excellent journalist. Your writing is terse, concise, and right to the point. Why don't you sign up for my journalism class next semester?"

I let out a sigh of relief. I knew he was the faculty adviser to our school's student newspaper, and in fact he even moonlighted as a copy editor at *The Denver Post.* Now he was inviting me to learn the skills of a reporter. How could I refuse?

I took his journalism class, started writing for the school paper, and eventually became its sports editor. During college, another instructor challenged me to write a personality feature and try to sell it to a real magazine. I was amazed when *Campus Life* actually sent me a check.

When I returned to my hometown a few years later to do a graduate degree at Denver Seminary, I got a night job on the copy desk at *The Denver Post* to help pay my bills. I walked in one night—and who should be sitting next to me editing stories for tomorrow's newspaper but Don Ridgway! His onetime student with no knack for descriptive paragraphs had become his journalistic colleague. Crusty Mr. Ridgway even smiled as we talked about that long-ago classroom conversation.

Today, more than forty years later, I continue to write. I still appreciate him for first pointing out what he saw me suited to do.

The Submarine Is All Yours

One of my dearest friends and hunting buddies for the last twenty-seven years is a former submarine commander, Captain Roy Springer. He graduated from the U.S. Naval Academy—and he, like Marshall, is a crack shot. One time jouncing along through the Colorado Rockies in my Jeep, I asked Roy if there was ever a moment in his life that prepared him to take on the challenging duties of commanding a submarine. I had heard and marveled at many of his "war stories" over the years, and I'd come to realize that leadership deep under the sea was a huge responsibility of technology, tactics, and nerve. Perhaps the greatest challenge of all was keeping a community of sailors living peacefully in those cramped quarters for long periods of time.

Roy thought for a moment (as he always does before answering a question), then smiled and replied, "I owe it all to my mother. I was very young playing in the sandbox just under her kitchen window." He went on to tell how the neighborhood kids tended to congregate in that sandbox each day. One time an argument broke out, kids were squabbling, and things were getting ugly. His mother, of course, had a front-row seat to the drama.

She finally heard enough, leaned out the window, and called down, "Now Roy, you get everybody happy out there, or you're coming in!"

Roy looked out my Jeep window and laughed. "Turns out, that was the most vital skill a submarine commander must have!"

"Spell My Name, Please"

If you could meet Dr. Joseph Kim, headmaster of Central Christian Academy in Suwon, Korea, you could not help being impressed. I have walked through the hallways of his multi-story school and come away in awe. I asked him once what propelled him to be a great teacher and now to surround himself with great teachers. Not surprisingly, there was a story at the very genesis of this brilliant educator.

First, a bit of background: Academics are a serious challenge to every young student in South Korea, but mercifully spelling isn't one of them. In the Korean language, there are no crazy irregularities, no "I before E except after C" nonsense, no "PH" that really sounds like "F" (or "GH" that doesn't sound at all in words like *through* and *fight*). If as a child you know the Korean alphabet, you know how to spell—everything. Words are spelled just as they sound.

So Joe was a competent, confident young student, except of course in English class when it came to spelling.

Then when he was in fourth grade, his family moved to the United States. He would have to attend an American school. Joe told me, "I vividly remember my first day. To my horror, my teacher, Mrs. Sharp, started out with spelling! She stood up in the front of the class with a stack of cards and began calling each student to stand beside their desk, one at a time. She would read the word from the next card, and the student had to spell it."

Even as Dr. Kim told me about this years later, I could hear the terrified nine-year-old boy in his voice. "Not only was I nervous in an unfamiliar classroom with strangers, but as my turn approached, I was ashamed. Ashamed of what I didn't know. Minute by minute, I realized I didn't know how to spell any of the words she was reading out." As the approaching tidal wave of certain humiliation crept his way, Joey watched and prayed for the second hand on the clock to speed up so the recess bell would ring and rescue him. His stomach was in knots, his mouth dry.

Despite his desperate prayers, Joey's turn came at last. "Mrs. Sharp saw me, pausing for what seemed an eternity. My heart pounded wildly. Then suddenly her face softened. 'Joseph, please stand and come up here to the front,' she said. *What?* My heart sank. This was the worst. I was embarrassed enough already. I was sure my Korean face was beet-red.

"The next seconds were a blur. Somehow I managed on wobbly legs to get myself to the front of the class. Mrs. Sharp announced, 'Boys and girls, Joey is going to spell his word a different way—on the blackboard. People in different countries use different letters to spell words. Now you will see what I mean.'

> **"She knew not only how to teach but how to love and care for the spirit of a child."**

"Then she gave me my word. It was her name, *Sharp*. 'Please write this in Korean,' she instructed."

Young Joey could hardly believe his sudden good fortune. "I turned and wrote confidently, 샤프. The chalk clicked noisily on the blackboard in a staccato. As I turned around, I saw a sea of waving hands, each student wanting me to spell their name in Korean. The bell soon rang for recess. I was swarmed by my new classmates poking their notebooks toward me, asking me to write their names. I spent the rest of the day like a sports or movie star, autographing everyone's books and notebooks with Korean letters."

In a minute, little Joey had been transformed from the awkward new kid with an Asian face to the class hero. At one point in the swarm of new friends, he looked up and met the teary eyes of Mrs. Sharp. The moment is sealed in his heart to this day. "She was more than just an expert teacher, a technician in the trade of teaching," he says. "She was a parent . . . even a pastor to me. She knew not only how to teach but how to love and care for the spirit of a child."

That day in spelling class, in a moment, an educator was born. His influence is felt today all across South Korea. He sits on the board of the worldwide Association of Christian Schools International. He has clearly found his calling. And it all started before recess that first day back in fourth grade.

Words, Deeds—or Both

Whether by word or by action—or both—the power of a moment to guide a child toward purpose or calling in life is amazing. Hermann Einstein said little, but the gift of that compass launched little Albert's scientific mind, for which we are all grateful. It was the grand sweep of Bil Keane's arm that spoke value into young Glen. The frightening crash of a prison door echoing down the cold walls of a cell block reverberated for years in the heart of little Alfred Hitchcock, spawning many a tale of terror.

In fact, what is done frequently trumps what is said. It is often the quiet actions that win the day for good or ill. This should come as an encouragement to the strong, quiet types among us who aren't so sure that they would know exactly the right words to say when the "just a minute" moment arrives. Words may not be what is called for in that moment at all. Maybe it's a life of integrity lived consistently in front of a child that will have the profound impact on the keen little witness who's watching. You never know when you are making a memory.

Walking the talk is the needed magic to help a child make their way in the world today.

Conclusion

WHAT NOW?

The story is told of Abraham Lincoln attending a church service in Washington, D.C. As he shook the preacher's hand on the way out, the reverend said, "Well, Mr. President, what did you think of my sermon?"

"It was fine," replied Lincoln, "but you didn't ask me to do anything great."

I don't want to make that mistake as we come to the conclusion of this journey together. I hope that inside your heart, you've been stirred anew by the realization that minutes matter—especially when the clay of our spirits is soft and impressionable during that amazing, once-in-a-lifetime phase called childhood.

Along the way I have read some of these stories and laughed out loud. At other times I have just dropped the manuscript to my lap, leaned back, and given way to tears. But we come now to our own "minute." We decide now, at this fork in the road, whether we will finish reading, sigh, put this book on the shelf, and forget about it . . . or whether we will pause and say, "Okay, that changes things. I don't want to just go back to being the same person who started this book. I don't want my heart, now awakened to the power of a moment, to just fall back asleep. I can't be the same as I was." The decision is yours and yours alone.

These pivotal moments come seldom in life. If you are blessed enough to live out your full "threescore and ten years," you will have been given, from birth to death, the gift of nearly 37 million minutes. Most rush by in a

blur as the years flow. But some, maybe just a handful, stand out like bea-
cons in the darkness, forever etched in your memory, defining who you are
and what you do. This could be one.

Sometimes, thanks to the media, we share memorable moments together nationally and even globally. I vividly remember dropping my
hammer in ninth-grade wood shop class when the school's loudspeakers

I cannot give to others what I do not have myself.

suddenly crackled with the shocking news that
President John F. Kennedy had been shot. I
recall sitting in the balcony of a Denver church
and watching on a big screen the televised event
of Neil Armstrong making history by stepping
onto the surface of the moon. I can still see the wall of television sets in
Sears as the *Challenger* shuttle blasted off into space that January morning in 1986—a minute of great pride and joy, followed instantly by horror
and despair. And who doesn't know exactly where they were the moments
the hijacked planes smashed into the World Trade Center towers on 9/11?

Such significant memories are pressed deeply into our hearts, and we
hold them collectively. These moments mattered; they had lasting, history-
changing impact. But deep within each of us resides our very own personal
moments, often known only to us.

First Things First: Remembering Your Own Moments

The first step on the journey forward is to pause and remember the
"just a minute" moments of our own lives. Before eagerly reaching out to
others, I may need to start by reaching back into myself. I cannot, after all,
give to others what I do not have myself. I cannot pass on what I have not
received. The safety announcements on a plane (even though we never pay
attention) are right: "Put on your own oxygen mask first; then help your
child with theirs."

So, whom do you owe? Who believed in you before you believed in
yourself? What did they say or do? Perhaps events have jumped to the
forefront of your mind as you've read the stories in this book. Maybe you
can recall many, or maybe just one. If you have drawn a complete blank in

recalling a moment good or bad, do not despair.

Not long ago I was on a speaking tour through Indonesia. At breakfast the first morning, I shared the "just a minute" concept with one of Compassion's Asian leaders. He is a brilliant, scholarly man. Raymond sat across from me pensively for a few moments and then said softly, "I don't think I have any such moments in my life."

As the trip moved from island to island, one morning he arrived at breakfast with a sparkle in his eye. "I've got one!" he said, beaming. He then told of his grandmother, a dear little Chinese lady who had received no schooling at all. She couldn't even make a phone call because she had never learned numbers. But she was a hardworking woman with a generous heart.

Raymond remembered that at one point when his family had fallen on hard times, she quietly stepped in and carried them financially for several years. She was a woman of action and few words, so when she did speak, her words had power in the boy's spirit. "Raymond, you are never so poor that you can't help others," she told him.

That moment imprinted his mind and values. It ultimately led him to his ministry to impoverished children through Compassion International. The memory of that moment had grown dim, but in retrospect, it was pivotal in this leader's heart for people in need.

The next morning, Raymond's memory had unearthed another gem: his high school history teacher, who had inspired his class at the end of each day's lesson as they trooped out of his room by saying, "You must have a dream, not for yourself but for a larger good!" Again, with those words echoing in his heart, he had chosen a life of service to others.

It got to be a regular breakfast joke as we continued to travel together: "So Raymond, what nugget have you remembered today?"

Not being able to immediately bring any moments to mind may be where you are right now. Give yourself time. Our world is in a great rush. We tend to focus eagerly on life in front of us, as through the windshield of a car. Whether it's risk, danger, worry, or opportunity that drives us, our instinct is to look forward. We live in a society obsessed with the next thing.

And that works most of the time. But every once in a while, even if just to be a prudent and safe driver, we need to glance backwards and see what lies behind us. Precious people, whom we owe dearly for our lives, can be left in the dust, tiny images lost in the rearview mirrors of our lives. I think that is why God calls on us to "Be still, and know that I am God" (Psalm 46:10). He is God of the present and the future to be sure. But He is also the God of our past. Moses, grasping that, prayed, "Teach us to number our days, that we may gain a heart of wisdom" (Psalm 90:12).

We don't need to be looking in the rearview mirror all that often. At the breakneck speed of daily life, it seems safer to keep our hands tight on the steering wheel and our eyes riveted on the road ahead. But if we will take the time for even a brief glance backward, we might be surprised to see with new eyes some once-forgotten moments we would do well to re-capture. Life-altering minutes. The spark of a dream that became a reality and shaped your life . . . or perhaps, sadly, one you have regretted every day since. We all have stories that explain who we are, why we do what we do—moments that, step by step, create and build our lives.

Examination Time

For some, to remember childhood memories or pivotal moments may require a personal appointment with yourself, a session or two of just you! Such quiet moments of introspection have to be intentional. They are nearly extinct in our crazy, fast-paced lives. But they are so worth it, poten-tially life-changing, if you will take the time.

Once I was trapped in seat 37A on a nine-hour international flight from Europe to Africa. The man in 37B was enormous. His size demanded more real estate than his seat could offer, so he occupied a good bit of 37A. I was so squashed that I ate my snack with my elbows literally touching each other. Forget about trying to get any work done in those cramped condi-tions. The plane's video system was broken. Outside my window the scen-ery never changed—just a two-toned vista of sky blue and the sandy tan of the Sahara Desert below. This flight seemed endless!

Funny what it can take for God to get our undivided attention. I had the strange feeling that I was being watched. I looked around and then realized who was looking at me: It was *me* looking back at myself in the reflection of the lifeless gray video screen on the back of the seat ahead. Now, men, you will understand how weird this was. We guys don't often stare at ourselves, at least not for very long, and certainly not in public. It's usually just long enough to scrape off our whiskers, brush our teeth, and run a comb through our hair. Done! Now, you ladies do have license to look at yourselves longer, attending to your hair, makeup, and clothing. And I think I speak for all mankind when I say we are grateful that you do. You make the world so much more beautiful with your presence. We (real) men know that we don't add all that much beauty, and most of us are just fine with that.

But there I was trapped in 37A. The giant beside me was asleep, and no one could see what I was doing. So I actually looked at myself. I studied my face as if it was that of a stranger. Really? Where had all those wrinkles suddenly come from? Was that an actual wattle hanging under my chin? Graying hair—when? What caused that?

Then my appointment with myself began. So, who is that guy? Where is he going? Why does he look so tired? What does he really care about? Why? When did he start being this person? What does he love? Hate? What frightens him? What does his future hold?

I reflected back . . . Who matters to him? Whom does he owe for his heart, spirit, mission, passion? Who believed in that little boy before he believed in himself? Who blessed him? Who almost destroyed him? How central is God in his life? Does heaven really await him a few breaths or heartbeats from now?

In time (and I had plenty of it for a change), I came to actually care about that guy in the video screen. As my mind wandered back over the years, I smiled, laughed, gritted my teeth, and shed quiet tears. It was a time I will never forget and always treasure.

So have you ever actually done that? No, I didn't think so. But at the start of this journey, perhaps you should. As you commit to reach out to others, reach out first to yourself—that little boy or girl looking back at you all grown up, but still deep inside a vulnerable, precious child . . . you.

Make an appointment with yourself. Ask yourself the questions I asked myself. I guarantee, you've got unrecognized heroes in your rearview mirror to whom you owe a lot, maybe your very life.

The Journey from There to Here

As memories begin to come, jot them down quickly so you won't forget later. Then pick one that stands out—who, what, when, where? Why did it matter? How were you affected by it? Has it made you a better person? Or has it wounded you deeply?

Have you spent a lifetime lifted up by the joy of that moment or struggling to overcome its hurt and pain? Did you give in and simply accept those hurtful words or actions? Did that moment build your life, or did it forever steal a bit of your heart, your spirit, your life?

Have tissues ready, because the story of that moment lifted you up or tore you down, and your heart will be fully engaged either way, maybe like never before. Your eyes may well up with tears of gratitude or perhaps sorrow or regret. Let them flow. For once, be totally honest with yourself. Nobody sees you or hears you, and there is nobody around to impress. That's just you looking back at you—you are that little child again, if only for a moment. You may have forgotten it or avoided it all these years. But for now, walk back into it, breathe it, feel it. It is yours and yours alone.

Give Thanks

For joyous memories, give thanks. First of all to God, who orchestrated your life to bring you to that uplifting moment. Then to that thoughtful, generous person who, in a minute, launched your life. Does that person even know what they did? Have you ever told them, reminding them of their kindness and the significance of their action in your life? Have you told them how you have passed their thoughtfulness on and the ripples that you know have gone out from their little pebble splash in your life? What you have done because of that moment?

If you have not, do it! Make it your mission to find them and thank them. Google them, do a Facebook search, seek them out, meet them, call them, or write them. If they are no longer alive, talk to their children! Often I have found these heroes may not even remember their act of kindness. You may be but one of a long line of people they have blessed along the way. No matter, tell them anyway. Watch the joy it brings them to know of the waves of goodwill that spread from their actions. If you will do this, I promise, you are on the brink of a wonderful, heartwarming, life-changing experience.

It is the desire of my heart that together we can start a tidal wave of gratitude, kindness, and goodness. Let it begin in the quiet of your heart, spill over to those you owe for your life, and inspire others to be alert and sensitive to the little ones—the next generation all around us who are waiting their turn to be blessed.

The Power of Forgiveness

Some of the memories you have resurrected may be excruciating. A wound, long buried in the recesses of your mind, still festers. You feel pain, rejection, shame, and anger. You feel you owe that person nothing. They added nothing to your life journey except hurt and sorrow. It has taken you many years to exorcise them and their actions from your still-damaged heart. I know about such hurt; my memory can still smell the scent of my scorched flesh from that candle—and not just my little fingers, but also my very heart.

I agree with Winn Collier: "To be healed for our future, we must be honest about our past." For those of us with these types of hurtful memories, the choice of whether to reconnect with the person who hurt us so deeply is more complex. It can only be answered by our own hearts. If it can be of any help, let me simply share what I did with my painful memories—I

> **I took a deep breath and went on:** *So, I forgive you—now get out! Get out of my heart. Get out of my mind. Get out of my life!*

forgave. Wait, don't abandon me yet; let me explain. I was a very wounded seventeen-year-old when I faced my demons.

Sitting around a fire with my fellow campers at Woodbine Ranch in Colorado, a "moment" arrived that changed my life yet again. The speaker that night was Glen Ruby. I don't remember much of what he said, but I recall him saying gently that some of us had people in our lives who had hurt us deeply by something they said or did to us. He suddenly had my full attention! He went on to say that although that pain and anger was destroying our spirits even years later, there was a good chance that the person who had hurt us wasn't bothered by it at all. Maybe they didn't even remember damaging us, or had minimized or rationalized it in their own minds as if it were nothing. The only one carrying the load and paying the price was us. We were allowing them to live "rent free" in our hearts, dominating our lives.

The only way forward, Glen explained, was to forgive. The words that warm summer evening rang true in my long-broken heart. So I gritted my teeth and said to myself, *Okay, you people—I know you aren't sorry for what you did to me all those years. I know I will never hear you ask for forgiveness. So I choose to forgive you anyway. I refuse to carry you any further in my life. You stole the joy of my childhood; I will not give you the rest of my life. You ruined my past, but I will not let you have my future.*

You will never forget what you will not forgive.

Through the smoke and the blur of my tears I took a deep breath and went on: *So, I forgive you—now get out! Get out of my heart. Get out of my mind. Get out of my life!* I know it was not a very gracious spirit of forgiveness . . . perhaps you understand . . . but in the depths of my broken spirit, it was all I was able to muster at the time.

Forgiveness is a very hard thing to do. It can be painful, maybe more painful than the original act that is being forgiven. I have since learned much more about it. Forgiveness does not mean that what that person did to you was okay or didn't matter. It doesn't mean you have to reconcile or reconnect with that hurtful person and bring them back into your life again. But it does mean you have to unclench your fists and give up your desire for revenge.

"Forgive and forget," the saying goes. But I have found it's not that simple. You never truly forget the deep hurts. But I know this: You will never forget what you will not forgive.

So, to those of us with damaged, deeply wounded spirits, the question of contacting that person again is a very personal decision. I chose not to. I chose that campfire minute to turn the page and, by God's grace, move forward with my life.

But a few years ago, I did choose to seek out and thank the campfire speaker, Glen Ruby. I found him living in California. He had been a schoolteacher all his life and now, in the waning years of his career, taught tough inner-city Los Angeles youth only occasionally, as a substitute teacher.

Over lunch, I learned that he really couldn't remember that evening or even his message delivered long ago across the sparks and the smoke. But he had heard of me, and he loved Compassion International.

I told him my painful story and in particular about his crucial moment in it: how God had redeemed my life, blessing me and many thousands of children through the ministry I now lead. Across the table, Glen's eyes filled with tears. "Wess," he said in a broken whisper, "that might have been the most important thing I ever did—the most important moment of my life!"

I smiled warmly at my hero and said, "I doubt it, Glen. I suspect I am just one of many, many children whom you profoundly touched. But I know this: It was one of the most important moments of my life. Thank you!"

Pay It Forward, Pass It On

Once you have come to grips with your own "just a minute" memories, it is time to reach out to the children God brings into your life. You have been equipped with your own childhood journey, either building on the positive or overcoming the negative, good or bad, to bless any child God places before you . . . even for just a minute.

So here is where I ask you to do something great: Bless the children!

You don't need another day of training. You, having been a child yourself, know all you need to know. You know deep in your heart what is needed. You know how adult contact feels if done right, and you may know how horribly wrong it can go if done poorly. Your mission begins with the very next child you encounter. What you do doesn't have to be profound, just loving. It doesn't have to last a lifetime—but it might.

They say it takes twenty-one days to make a new behavior into a habit, a regular part of your life. Those of us in the perpetual quest to work out and get in shape know very well how hard this is to get started and actually do. So if you are like me, you need a way to remember what you've committed to do.

I wear a Mickey Mouse watch. That's right. The CEO of a multinational organization wears a child's watch. Why? Because it helps me not take myself too seriously. More importantly, it helps me remember my commitment to children. Every time I glance at my watch, I remember. If there is a child in the vicinity, I find a way to do something to brighten their day, even if it's just a wave, a smile, a compliment, a joke, or a hug. If there are no children around, I just breathe a prayer for children. It's part of my worldview, my calling, my makeup. Yes, I'm a professional—but so are you!

Bloom Where You're Planted

Certain children are going to be brought into your path as you set out on the quest to bless them. Some will be the children in your home, or the homes of those in your family. Next there will be children who are not relatives, but still a regular part of your life—kids in your neighborhood, school, church, and town that you see frequently. Then there are the "one-timers," children you have never seen before and may never see again. But they are a part of your life or, better yet, you are a part of their lives, maybe for "just a minute."

With our very own children, we have the luxury of knowing them well and spending many minutes living with them. Still, we need to be alert to seize the magically teachable moments that happen along the way. We also can orchestrate strategic moments in our children's lives. We can know the spirits of our children well enough that we actually do the right thing at the right time in the right way! Or at least we try. In their powerful bestselling book *The 5 Love Languages of Children*, my friend Dr. Gary Chapman and coauthor Dr. Ross Campbell help us recognize how each of our children learns. Knowing this can help us prepare to speak the message at just the right time in a way they can best receive. It also may allow us to speak that message consistently over time as our children grow.

> **We solemnly pledged to each other that if God chose to bless us with children of our very own, we would not leave them behind in our passion to bless the hurting children of the world.**

But they emphasize that the most important thing a parent can do is provide their child with *unconditional love*—keeping their "love tank" full. Disciplining a child, educating a child, equipping that child for life—all depend on filling her with unconditional love and kindness, even moment by moment.

When my wife Donna and I were married thirty-two years ago in a little church in Haiti, we knew even then that we were going to give our lives in service to children living in poverty across the world. But we solemnly pledged to each other that if God chose to bless us with children of our very own, we would not leave them behind in our passion to bless the hurting children of the world. We determined never to hear these words from the mouths of our children: "You cared about all the kids of the world, but you forgot about me!"

It turns out God honored that commitment and granted us two sweet-spirited, godly young ladies who love the children of the world as much as their parents do. I have worked far harder at being a good papa to them than being a good president for Compassion. As I write this, I am still my two daughters' favorite "toy." All grown up now, we are best friends.

All that to say, the first place to engage in sacred moments is right in your own home, with the little ones God has specifically entrusted to you.

Are Your Children "Impressed"?

The concept of a child's spirit being like soft clay was first stated by God Himself in Deuteronomy 6. Who would know the makeup of a child better than the child's own Creator? The very hands that tenderly knit all little babies in their mothers' wombs (Psalm 139) are the hands that carved the Ten Commandments into the stone tablets and delivered them to Moses on Mount Sinai (Deuteronomy 5). In the very next chapter, just days later, perhaps mindful of the spirit of a child, God announced a summary of the Law that even a child's heart could understand: "Love the Lord your God with all your heart and with all your soul and with all your strength" (Deuteronomy 6:5).

Then God delivered an "Eleventh Commandment" to adults. It makes the "soft clay" point clearly: "Impress these on your children." *Impress* means to gently press something into a pliable surface until it leaves a permanent mark. This mark will last as the clay begins to harden in youth and become rock-hard in adulthood. The thought comes through again in the well-known verse "Start children off on the way they should go, and even when they are old they will not turn from it" (Proverbs 22:6).

God seems so determined that the parents get this assignment and do it right that He explains in detail how and when it is to be done. "Seize the moments," He says. "Talk about [My instructions] when you sit at home and when you walk along the road, when you lie down and when you get up" (Deuteronomy 6:7). In other words, every minute matters!

Beyond seizing the moments spontaneously, our own daughters allowed us to make deliberate impressions. Wanting to impress kindness and respect for those in need in America, and not just overseas, we established some family traditions of kindness.

For instance, on Thanksgivings, to impress on Jenny and Katie that this day was indeed about gratitude and that not everyone was as blessed on that day as we were, we made a tradition of volunteering with Silver Key's "Meals on Wheels" program. It involved delivering meals to elderly and homebound people of Colorado Springs. We would plot our assigned twenty homes on a city map. As we loaded our car with meals, we would pray for the people we would meet, and again before we walked up their sidewalks. Each was a divine appointment poised to impress the spirits of our girls.

Some people would just meet us at the door and take the food with a quick thank-you. But others, the lonely ones, would invite us inside to visit a moment. We met some amazing people—an elderly ballerina, a wounded Army sniper—at the lowest points in their lives. My girls learned to listen respectfully, ask engaging questions, joke a bit, compliment, encourage, pray, and leave with a warm embrace, having found a new friend, a new perspective, and a new gratitude on Thanksgiving Day.

The most precious thing a parent can give their child is a warm memory. And like this one, some can be deliberately, intentionally, lovingly crafted to deliver magic moments.

I am pretty sure that when God said to impress His laws "on your children," He didn't mean just the nuclear family. He surely meant the extended family, the whole "village" it took to raise the children. That had to include grandparents, who have a unique role of their own to play.

In this rush-around, high-tech world where grandchildren huddle over gadgets and electronic games, grandparents may begin to feel a bit irrelevant to their family's little ones. But you are not! As busy and overwhelmed as their parents may be, you are one of the few lasting, endearing, face-to-face, heart-to-heart message bearers your grandchildren still have in their lives. Your stories, memories, and loving words will always cut through the clutter of the electronic din and be especially powerful. So deliberately pray over, ponder, and prepare for those teachable moments at Christmas, Thanksgiving, and birthdays. Such magical moments will inevitably be remembered deep in the heart of a child.

My parents had a huge impact on their four granddaughters when one Christmas, Grandpa declared, "From now on, Grandma and I don't want any more presents! Instead of you doing things for us, we want to know what you have done for others." In the midst of the wrapping paper, empty gift boxes, and toys all around, that was a powerful, teachable moment.

From that time forward, the granddaughters focused throughout the year on doing acts of kindness for others and documenting them in scrapbooks that they would happily present to their grandparents on Christmas morning after all the other presents were opened and stowed. One by one I watched those little girls climb into their grandparents' laps and tell them what they had done for others. They loved their grandparents dearly and were delighted to see the joy and pride in their eyes. I was deeply grateful to my parents for these precious moments in which they affirmed my daughters and gently shaped their little hearts.

Grandparents, if you think you can't compete with the hustle and bustle of your grandchildren's lives, if you think you are done, if you believe nobody really needs you or listens to you anymore—your greatest mission may be NOW, and still to come!

Imagine Thanksgiving meals where grandparents, aunts, and uncles agree ahead of time to tell their stories of the positive "just a minute" moments for the children to hear. The family history, tales of gratitude, laughter, values affirmed, and kindness shown just might show them a side of the family they would otherwise never see. It just might bring about "minutes" of their own. If a child jumps in with a story, give them the right-of-way!

Birthdays are natural milestones in which "just a minute" memories can easily happen. Why not make it a family tradition to speak a bedtime blessing over the child? Start off with a bedtime story, a "once upon a time" about a strong prince or a beautiful princess that morphs into *their* story. See how long it takes for them to say, "Hey, Mommy, you're telling *my* story. That's me!" Then laugh and tell them how much you love their story. The things you've watched them do. How proud you are of them. How much you love who they are and who they are becoming. How blessed you feel to get to be their parents. Finally, encourage them for the coming year, and pray a prepared prayer of blessing.

Widen the Circle

Next we move to other children who are regularly in your life in one way or another. You don't have the advantage of hours and hours with them, but they are a part of your world, and your impact on them can be huge.

After I had written *Too Small to Ignore,* I did a promotional tour to get the message of that book out through television, radio, magazines, events, and speaking engagements. One day I was in Little Rock, Arkansas, for a radio interview with Dennis Rainey and Bob Lepine for FamilyLife. Just before we went on the air, the program's producer, a woman named Tonda Nations, came into the studio.

"Wess," she said, "we read and talk about a lot of books on this program. But I want you to know that yours was one of the few that moved me so deeply I just had to go out and do something. It changed my mind, my heart, and my behavior."

She went on to tell me a wonderful story. Tonda said she lived on a quiet street where, for some reason, the neighborhood children always seemed to choose her driveway as their favorite place to gather and play. She had noticed that one girl always seemed to be left out of the games. She seemed a little different, shunned by the other children. She often spent the evening sitting quietly by herself, rarely talking or joining in.

"So, last night your book inspired me to actually reach out and do something about that little girl. As I stepped out of my house to take my usual evening walk, I stooped down beside her and said, 'I'm going for a walk around the block. Wanna come?'"

The girl looked up, surprised. "Really? Yes, I'd love to. Can I, can I?" She jumped up excitedly.

She fairly skipped in her joy as she danced, laughed, and guided her new friend around the block. "Those flowers are brand-new," she said. "Two days ago they were just little green buds." A little further along around the corner Tonda's escort offered a secret. "That's Buddy," she said, pointing to a dog barking behind a picket fence. "He thinks it's his job to act tough, but he's just a sweetie. Watch!" She slipped her fingers through the slats and got an enthusiastic lick from a dog wriggling from head to toe like he had two tails—gone from wolf to poodle, his cover blown. "Don't worry, Buddy; your secret is safe with us," she assured him.

Tonda's eyes sparkled as she told me about being shown birds' nests, a cat's favorite hiding place in a patch of flowers, the rediscovered scent of newly mowed grass—all through the delighted eyes of a child. "It was like I had never been around that block before."

That was six years ago. I called Tonda as I was writing this book and asked her about her little neighbor. "She's not so little anymore," Tonda said, "but we are still good friends. Now on our walks, it's my turn to escort. She's a young lady with all the trials of finding her way through the heartaches and challenges of growing up. I listen, laugh, cry, hug, and pray, doing my best to help her. It kinda feels like we've gone full circle."

My question to you is this: Could you do that? *Would* you do that? Why not make a list of the children who are a part of your life on a somewhat regular basis? Who are they?

Then ask yourself: What are they going through? Is there something you could plan to do to show kindness and maybe launch a just-a-minute moment? Imagine the blessing in the world if you did that . . . if we all did!

Caring for Even the Caregivers

Caring for children day in and day out is difficult, exhausting, exasperating, and often thankless work no matter who you are and how much you love the children. I so admire teachers and mothers who give themselves so selflessly to the little ones in their care. How very wrong that they are often the least recognized, rewarded, or affirmed by our society while they are doing probably the most significant work of all. If in our mission to bless children we are really paying attention, we will note that never far from the little ones are these amazing caregivers. They're easy to spot by their rumpled clothes, disheveled hair, and bags under their eyes!

Sometimes the heroes who are consistently making those magic moments happen for children are themselves in need of being picked up and given a "moment" of encouragement. Awhile back I was sitting on a bench waiting for my car to get through the car wash. On the bench next to me was a young mother with her maybe three-year-old son. They were chatting about the things around them as if they were old friends. I sat there listening to the heart-to-heart conversation between this grown woman and this young child.

When their car was ready, they stood up to go to it. I said to the young mother, "Excuse me, but can I just take a second to tell you that you are doing a wonderful job raising that boy. I've heard a bit of your conversation, and he is a very lucky boy to have a mom like you."

She smiled and said, "Do you really think so?"

They walked off hand in hand toward their car . . . until the young mom suddenly stopped in her tracks. She then turned and came back. With tears welling up in her eyes, she said, "Thank you—can I give you a hug? Nobody has ever told me that before. I'm trying so hard to be a good mother."

> **Some of you may decide that caring for caregivers is going to be a big part of your "just a minute" commitment.**

She was a genuine hero, much like other moms, teachers, babysitters, Sunday school teachers, coaches, club leaders, nurses, and camp counselors. And some of these are men as well. They all deserve our notice and applause.

Some of you may decide that caring for caregivers is going to be a big part of your "just a minute" commitment. You may notice that almost always within arm's reach of every little child is a joyful, or harried, caregiver. You don't have to search hard for these people.

I travel a lot on airplanes, and those metal tubes we cram ourselves into and sit for hours on end are torture chambers for the little ones among us—and so naturally for their moms and dads. I make it my habit to rarely pass a small child on these interminable journeys without a word of encouragement. If the child is being a little angel, it is easy to let them know how good they are! If they are being miserable, there's the equal opportunity to breathe a word of encouragement to the frustrated parent: "Been there, done that—don't give up. This chapter passes. Really, life goes on! Can I help in any way?" Men, there is no excuse for a young mother to struggle down the Jetway or aisle with all the tons of accouterment that traveling with a child requires. Jump up and lend a hand . . . and a smile.

Needless to say, the same moments can arise in the grocery store, the mall, at church, or anywhere else you find a child.

I Was a Stranger . . . and in "Just a Minute" You Took Me In

Now we move on to a new part of the adventure. What about the children who are neither your own nor a regular part of your life—the little "one-timers" whom God brings across your path maybe only once and maybe for just a minute? Can any lifelong impact or memories be made that quickly? Absolutely—we've seen them all through this book.

Remember my friends at the Denver airport shoeshine stand? I told them as I was writing this book that I was going to tell their heroic moment with that "marching shoes" boy earlier. They were delighted. Then the other day as I climbed into the chair again, A.J. looked up. "Wess!" he exclaimed. "We were just talking about you this morning." He then told me of a Polish businessman, traveling with his five-year-old daughter, who needed his shoes shined just an hour or so earlier. His little girl was bored and restless. A.J. suddenly had an idea. He asked the child if she wanted to help him shine her daddy's shoes. Putting on the plastic gloves, she was giggling and ready. Together A.J. and the girl meticulously shined the shoes of a now-smiling businessman.

When it was all done, A.J. gave the little girl a dollar for helping him and for doing such a good job. Needless to say, A.J. got a big tip from a grateful father. Off they walked, now hand in hand, the little girl skipping along and chattering excitedly. A.J. said, "We thought, *Wess would be so proud of us.* And suddenly here you are!"

Oh, how I long for a world where all of us could act with that spirit—alert to the children around us, ready to take a moment to lift them up as they cross our paths! If you have made it this far in this book, you are someone with the kind of heart who could make this your mission. On behalf of the little ones who cannot speak for themselves, I ask you to join me in this. We really can make this world a better place. As trite as the expression has become, it is still true: It happens one child at a time, and moment by moment.

Beware, a Cloud of Witnesses

The truth is, we are all actively engaged in impacting the lives of children, whether we realize it or not. We are daily surrounded by a cloud of witnesses who are watching our lives, many of them children. You never know when you are being watched by a child! This moment happened to me many years ago when I was living in Haiti, by far the poorest country in our Western Hemisphere.

"Msie, eske ou Jezu?" ("Mister, are you Jesus?") The question from the little Haitian lad I had just met on the grimy streets of Port-au-Prince startled me. I was no newcomer to this overwhelming, impoverished city, and I could tell the boy was no streetwise con artist. The sincerity in his dark eyes cautioned me to not take his inquiry lightly. But what on earth could have prompted the question?

My mind retraced my steps since I had met little Jean Pierre earlier that morning. He had been sitting alone on the curb outside a KFC franchise. The street children often gathered there beneath the restaurant kitchen's exhaust vent. It blasted out the savory smell of fried chicken to mingle with the usual stench of urine and rotting garbage that filled the streets of the capital city. Jean Pierre was eating a crust of bread as I walked by. Our eyes met, and I paused in my errands to talk with him for a minute. He explained to me that "if you eat a crust of bread beneath these vents, it makes the bread taste like chicken." We shared a laugh, a hug, and I walked on. Jean Pierre followed me at a distance. I forgot about him and went about my business.

At Madam Sarah's corner, I bought a handful of peanuts for one *gourde* (twenty cents). As usual, I thanked her and walked off before she could finish digging in her basket to come up with change for my five-*gourde* bill. I gave the nuts to a man begging at the next corner. As on most days, I got my shoes shined four or five times. Not that they needed it, but it gave me a few precious moments with a child or an old man who needed a kind word and a few cents for their work. My car likewise was washed numerous times each day with the filthy water that ran down the street gutters. Each occasion gave me the excuse to joke with the child who graced me with his industriousness. A generous tip, a hug, an exaggerated admiration at the splendor of my "shiny" car, and a word about his being the very best car washer in all of the city . . . then I pressed on.

Jean Pierre had clandestinely taken all of this in and had come to the conclusion that a man who did these sorts of things must, in fact, be Jesus! What an honor! And, to those who know me well . . . what a mistake!

Seizing the moment, the boy and I walked back to KFC, bought chicken, then sat on the curb and talked about what Jesus was really like. I don't know, and won't know this side of heaven, if that was an eternal moment for Jean Pierre. Perhaps not; his parting words to me were "Thank you, mister. This chicken is delicious; it tastes just like bread." But the chance to move his imagination a bit closer to the Savior was well worth the time.

The Moment Is Now

In closing, I want to thank you for letting me be a small part of your life through this book. I have shared with you the very cry of my heart. Proverbs 31:8 says, "Speak up for those who cannot speak for themselves." That most certainly includes the little ones who live among us. It is within our grasp to shape the future, if we will.

Do you already have a mission that grips your heart and can move you to tears in thirty seconds?

The time is now, while their spirits are soft and impressions are easily made. Tomorrow's leaders, in whose hands the future rests, will still climb into your lap today, run to your embrace, laugh at your jokes, listen to your wisdom, and comfort you with tiny arms and big hugs. But not for long. In a few short years, the clay will harden, and they will inherit the corridors of power and start making the decisions that will shape our world.

So I'm asking you to join me in doing something great. Do you already have a cause, a passion, a mission that grips your heart and can move you to tears in thirty seconds? If not, you are not fully alive! If there isn't something in your life that is bigger than you, outside of you, not about you, that demands and deserves your time, talent, and treasure, I beg you, don't live like that. We don't have time to simply coast.

I invite you to join me in making this cause for children your own passion, to fight the battle child by child and minute by minute, being alert and willing to step in and make a memory that just might transform a life, heal a wounded heart, or lovingly send a child on their way. In the heart of a child, a moment can last forever. It is my prayer that a grassroots movement will arise, millions of us dedicated to recognize and seize these moments to breathe hope, joy, faith, life, and love into the little ones God has entrusted to us—maybe in just a minute!

Share your
Share

http://www

story.

your life.

Has someone spoken truth, love, compassion, or encouragement into your life in a way that has changed you forever? You can use your story to change a life!

When we share our stories, we share ourselves.

Join me in this exciting new initiative – **JustaMinute.com**. This new website will give you a chance to:

- Encourage others by telling the story of a person who has spoken truth into your life.
- Send e-cards to the people who have made an eternal difference in your life.
- Learn more about the people who have spoken truth into my life.

Share your story at **JustaMinute.com** and stand with thousands of others as a "great cloud of witnesses" for a world in need!

Wess Stafford

JustaMinute.com

Releasing children from poverty
Compassion®
in Jesus' name

THANK YOU

Just a Minute is about both recognizing and creating profound moments that touch and change lives. It is my hope and prayer that God will use you and me as His conduits for such moments in the lives of others, especially children. So I thank God in advance for the divine appointments He has already planned for us all, and for nudging us to recognize them and to *carpe diem!*

I have been blessed by many special moments and am indebted to those who believed in me long before I came to believe in myself. To the poor in the West African village of my childhood who gently shaped my heart and mind when my young spirit was like soft clay, I owe you my life. To those who have been models, teachers, and encouragers to me in my lifelong quest to speak up for those who cannot speak for themselves, this book has grown out of your influence in my life.

My deepest gratitude goes to my loving wife Donna, my rock and my North Star. So many of my most precious minutes have been lived at your side and wouldn't have been possible had you not, in one very special moment thirty-two years ago, committed to our partnership in life and ministry and then confirmed that vow in so many moments since. The many times over the years that I have been half a world away from you, it was my greatest joy and comfort to feel your love and support despite the divide. What a blessing to know that even when we cannot be together hand in hand, we are still "heart in heart," united in spirit. Thank you for your help on this project and so many others.

To our daughters Jenny and Katie: You endured many fatherless moments in your childhood in order to share me with the children of the world. May God bless you for that sacrifice and reward you as only He can. It takes just a minute for my eyes to well up with tears and my heart to overflow with our cherished family memories. I am so blessed to be your father and friend, so proud and thankful for the sweet-spirited, talented, witty, godly women you have become. Thank you for the precious moments you continue to tuck into my heart.

It has been my privilege for several decades to fight the battle for children alongside my Compassion International family. I've had a front-row seat to witness the truth that God honors those who honor Him. I am keenly aware that leadership is a gift given to the leader by those who commit to follow—what an honor it is for me to receive this gift from such extraordinary people. Thank you for bolstering me during so many writing moments by sending words of encouragement and assurances of your prayer support.

A very special acknowledgment to the heroes who serve on Compassion's board of directors and believed in this book from its genesis—thank you for not resting (nor letting me rest!) until we at last reached its revelation. Compassion's remarkable leadership team, under the competent guidance of David Dahlin, stepped up in order to let me step away for a season to write. Thank you for closing ranks and serving with excellence. To my executive assistant, Angie Lathrop: I am grateful for your cheerful dedication and tireless can-do spirit, despite the extra work this book brought across your desk. My thanks also to the rest of the outstanding president's office staff: Dinah Meyer, Mary Lou Elliott, Gayle Call, Ashley Higgins, Angelina Dieleman, and Dr. Scott Todd. We are not just coworkers but fellow soldiers and dear friends who laugh and cry together. I do not take for granted your generous support and your always rising to the occasion with heart and soul. Throughout the process of creating this book, I felt sustained by your love and your faithful prayer.

I am thankful to so many who caught the vision for this message and jumped in enthusiastically to tell me their stories and the stories of others. This book could have been twice as long had it contained all the treasures that were shared with me. Special thanks to Evelyn Gibson, Jim Sanders, Peggy Campbell, Katie Burke, and the staff at Ambassador Advertising—you were the first to understand my heart on this and encourage me. And to the Stepelton family—thank you for your gracious gift of a writing hideaway at your beautiful and inspiring North Carolina home. To Krissy Thomas Smith, Stephen Sorenson, and all of you across Twitter and Facebook who researched stories and also entrusted me with your own, both joyful and tragic, I am truly grateful.

I chose Moody Publishers out of respect and gratitude. This great publishing house's profits go right back into scholarships for the next generation of students at my alma mater, Moody Bible Institute. I grew up in a missionary family of modest means, and I know there was a minute in my life long ago when someone in the admissions office looked at a not-very-impressive college application and said, "Wess Stafford . . . it's a long shot, but let's give him a chance." My foundation of faith and life of service were set in motion thanks to someone else's generosity, and I will be eternally grateful. What a joy to give back in even a small way. Greg Thornton and Randall Payleitner listened to my vision for this book and immediately went "all in" (wait, I'm not sure I can use that term at Moody!). They, along with so many on the Moody team, gave this project their full commitment and did not rest until the job was done: a movement of love launched!

What a joy to partner once again with Dean Merrill. He is the most professional, dedicated, and disciplined writer I have ever known. His imagination caught the vision of tossing the pebble of this just-a-minute message into life's pond and watching the resulting ripples eventually create waves of blessing for children. That passion carried us both forward as deadlines loomed! Thank you, Dean, for your heart and for your exceptional expertise.

Finally, I am grateful to you, the readers. Those of you who read *Too Small to Ignore* and gently prodded me with "What else? What's next?"—the message of this book is a tribute to your desire to see the children of the world loved, protected, nurtured, and blessed. May this vision inspire us all to sow minutes of loving-kindness in the lives of every child we encounter.

NOTES

1. See Zechariah 3:2.

2. John Pollock, *Wesley: The Preacher*, a biography published by Kingsway Publications/David C Cook. Publisher permission required to reproduce. All rights reserved. Copyright © 1989, 2000, 15–16. By permission of David C. Cook.

3. Adapted from Charles R. Swindoll, *Sanctity of Life: The Inescapable Issue*, (Nashville: Word Publishing, 1990). © 1990 by Charles R. Swindoll, Inc. All rights reserved worlwide, by permission of Thomas Nelson.

4. Misti L. Kerl, "The Wave Game," *A Sixth Bowl of Chicken Soup for the Soul*, edited by Jack Canfield and Mark Victor Hansen. Copyright © 1998 by Misti Kerl. Reprinted with the permission of The Permissions Company, Inc., on behalf of Health Communications Inc., www.hcibooks.com, 190–92.

5. Tali Whiteley, "Green Journal" was adapted from "The Dustpan Carrier," *A Sixth Bowl of Chicken Soup for the Soul*, edited by Jack Canfield and Mark Victor Hansen. Copyright © 1998 by Tali Whiteley. Reprinted with the permission of The Permissions Company, Inc., on behalf of Health Communications Inc., www.hcibooks.com, 233–34.

6. Dan Clark, "Fervent Fan" was adapted from "Ron," *A Second Chicken Soup for the Women's Soul,* edited by Jack Canfield, Mark Victor Hansen, Jennifer Read Hawthorne, and Marci Shimoff. Copyright © 1998 by Dan Clark. Reprinted with the permission of The Permissions Company, Inc., on behalf of Health Communications Inc., www.hcibooks.com, 170–71.

7. Edgar Bledsoe, "Problem or Solution," *Chicken Soup for the Woman's Soul*, edited by Jack Canfield, Mark Victor Hansen, Jennifer Read Hawthorne, and Marci Shimoff. Copyright © 1996 by Edgar Bledsoe. Reprinted with the permission of The Permissions Company, Inc., on behalf of Health Communications Inc., www.hcibooks.com, 3–5.

8. John Toland, *Adolf Hitler* (New York: Doubleday, 1976), 12

9. Bob Kelley, compiler, *Worth Repeating* (Grand Rapids, Mich.: Kregel, 2003), 45.

10. James P. Lenfestey, "Throwing the Big One Back: a moral tale for the fishing opener," *Star Tribune*, May 15, 1988. Reprinted with permission.

11. Colin Powell with Joseph E. Persico, *My American Journey* (New York: Ballantine, 1995), 16–18.

12. Tony Dungy, *Quiet Strength* (Wheaton, Ill.: Tyndale, 2007), 12–13. Reprinted with permission.

13. E. Stanley Jones, *Victorious Living,* updated edition (Minneapolis: Summerside, 2010), November 27 entry.

14. Pamela J. deRoy, "Beautiful on the Inside," *A Fourth Course of Chicken Soup for the Soul,* edited by Jack Canfield, Mark Victor Hansen, Hanoch McCarty, and Meladee McCarty. Copyright © 1996 by Pamela deRoy. Reprinted with the permission of The Permissions Company, Inc., on behalf of Health Communications Inc., www.hcibooks.com, 30–33.

15. *A Third Serving of Chicken Soup for the Soul,* compiled by Jack Canfield and Mark Hansen (Deerfield Beach, Fla.: Health Communications Inc., 1996), 217–19.

16. Marsha Arons, "The White Gardenia," *Chicken Soup for the Woman's Soul,* edited by Jack Canfield, Mark Victor Hansen, Jennifer Read Hawthorne, and Marci Shimoff. Copyright © 1996 by Marsha Arons. Reprinted with the permission of The Permissions Company, Inc., on behalf of Health Communications Inc., www.hcibooks.com, 72–73.

17. Originally published in *Focus on the Family Magazine,* June 1994, 14.

18. Adapted from *The Winner Within* by Pat Riley, 1993 by Riley & Company, Inc. Used by permission of G. P. Putnam's Sons, a division of Penguin Group (USA) Inc.

19. Condensed from *The First Year of Teaching: Real World Stories from America's Teachers,* edited by Pearl Rock Kane. Copyright © 1991 by Pearl Rock Kane, editor. Reprinted by permission of Bloomsbury USA.

20. From *Mini Moments for Mothers* by Robert Strand. Copyright © 1996. Used with permission from New Leaf Publishing Group, Green Forest, Ark.

21. Jack Canfield, "Spilled Milk," was adapted from "Remember, We're Raising Children, Not Flowers," *A Second Helping of Chicken Soup*, edited by Jack Canfield and Mark Victor Hansen. Copyright © 1995 by Jack T. Canfield and

Hasen and Hansen LLC. Reprinted with the permission of The Permissions Company, Inc., on behalf of Health Communications Inc., www.hcibooks.com, 85–86.

22. Sandra P. Aldrich, *Bless Your Socks Off—Unleashing the Power of Encouragement* (Colorado Springs: Focus on the Family Publishing/Tyndale House, 1998), 18–20. Out of print, used by permission of author.

23. Walter Isaacson, *Einstein* (New York: Simon & Schuster, 2007), 13.

24. From *Long Walk to Freedom* by Nelson Mandela. Copyright © 1994, 1995 by Nelson Rolihlahla Mandela, Little. Brown and Company, 25–26. Used by permission of Hachette Book Group.

25. *A Testament of Hope: The Essential Writings and Speeches of Martin Luther King Jr.*, edited by James M. Washington (New York: HarperCollins, 1986), 420. Reprinted by arrangement with the Heirs to the Estate of Martin Luther King Jr, c/o Writers House as agent for the proprietor, New York, NY.

26. Carol Kline with Jean Harper, "The Wind Beneath Her Wings,"*Chicken Soup for the Woman's Soul,* edited by Jack Canfield, Mark Victor Hansen, Jennifer Read Hawthorne, and Marci Shimoff. Copyright © 1996 by Carol Kline. Reprinted with the permission of The Permissions Company, Inc., on behalf of Health Communications Inc., www.hcibooks.com, 222–25.

Grateful acknowledgement is expressed to those who have granted permission to include copyrighted materials in this book. Every effort has been made to contact those whose copyrighted material exceeds fair limits. Any inadvertent omission of credit will be gladly corrected in future editions.

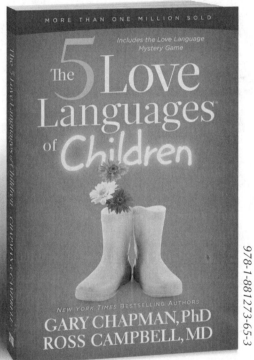

Sponsor a child and give them hope.

When you sponsor a child through Compassion International, your generosity provides Christian training, educational opportunities, and health care for a child living in extreme poverty. You can save a life on the other side of the world. Please sponsor a child today.

To receive more information, please either:
- Complete the postcard below, tear it out, and drop it in the mail
- Call toll-free **800–336–7676**
- Visit **Compassion.com**

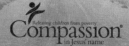

"You have the chance to launch a life."

Wess Stafford
President, Compassion International

compassion.com

☐ Yes, I'm interested in receiving more information on child sponsorship [KIT29].

YOUR NAME

Address

City   State   Zip

Phone Number

Email Address

121968